AGING, GENDER AND CRIME

SOCIAL PERSPECTIVES OF AGING

Jason L. Powell (Series Editor)

(Dean of Faculty, University of Liverpool, Liverpool, UK)

SOCIAL PERSPECTIVES OF AGING

AGING, GENDER AND CRIME

JASON L. POWELL

Nova Science Publishers, Inc.
New York

LIBRARY OF CONGRESS CATALOGING-IN-PUBLICATION DATA

Aging, gender and crime / editor, Jason L. Powell.
    p. cm.
  Includes index.
  ISBN 978-1-61942-150-9 (soft cover)
  1. Older people--Crimes against. 2. Older women--Crimes against. 3. Crime--Sociological aspects. I. Powell, Jason L., 1971-
  HV6250.4.A34A45 2011
  364.3--dc23
                      2011042515

Published by Nova Science Publishers, Inc. † *New York*

CONTENTS

PREFACE

This book explores the issue of crime and its relationship to gender and aging. This is a forgotten area of analysis in disciplines of criminology, gerontology and even in Feminist theorizing. This book begins by exploring the relationship of crime, aging and victimization. The book then moves to assess the main issues associated with understanding imprisonment for older people. The book focuses its attention on gender and the relationship withmental health and institutional psychiatric care.

The final part of the book explores the issue of theorizing aging and relationship to crime.

Chapter 1

PROBLEMATIZING OLD AGE, VICTIMIZATION AND CRIME

BACKGROUND

'Crime is perceived to be an age war, with young offenders preying on innocent older victims...Politicians have quickly, and quite unjustifiably, identified the elderly as particularly vulnerable to crime' (Mawby, 1988:101).

'Old age is shamefully seen like head lice in children and venereal disease in their older siblings'(Stott, 1981: 3).

This paper explores old age as an important sociological dimension of analysis and dissects its relationship to victimization and contemporary crime. The article is concerned with examining how the notion of victim applies to older people within the life-course. We then move to explore the relationship between old age and victimization and highlight a number of implications for the study of age and its relationship to victimization. We conclude by suggesting that current political discourses position the concept of 'victim' along neo-liberal lines of 'responsibility' as opposed to the societal construction of the victim. In recent years, the experiences of 'age groups' across the life-course have been taken as a developing issue of concern in Criminology (Powell, 2001). While this has been the case regarding 'younger people', the criminological development of ideas pertaining to the experiences and representations of 'older people' has been 'unchartered territory' (Brogden and Nijar, 2000). Indeed, when comparing the category of 'age' to the criminological research that covers race, class and gender; age has been hidden and seen as secondary importance. The major issue is perceived as being how to overcome the sociological triumvirate of race, class and gender without ignoring the experiences of individuals based on other equally important variables such as age, disability and sexuality. Our aim is to demonstrate that researchers studying the relationship between older people and victimization would benefit from a more careful conceptualization of 'age', one which focuses on the ways in which 'old age' itself is socially constructed, is represented and used by particular interest groups.

We must question how relevant old age is to the process of victimization. But before we do that, we will map out what is meant by the concept. In western societies, an individuals' age is counted on a chronological or numerical foundation, beginning from birth to the current point of age, or when an individual has died. It is only by deconstructing age in the study of criminology and victimology that we can begin to see how and why such disciplinary discourses construct the notion of 'aging' in relation to the victim.

Counting age is a social construction because it is a practice underpinned by conceptions of time in regional, national and global spaces, which came to be of increasing importance with the historical development of industrial capitalism (Phillipson, 1982). The concept of 'age' has three main focal points: first, age and aging have a biological and physiological dimension, so that over time and space, the appearance of physical bodies change (Moody, 1998); second, the aging of an individual takes place within a particular period of time and space; third, as individuals, society has a number of socially defined expectations how people of certain ages are supposed to behave and how they are positioned via gender, social class and ethnicity. 'Old age' is difficult to define, the legal concept of 'pensionable age' has been defined as 'old age' (Biggs, 1993); those people requiring care management have been predominantly those older people aged 70 and over (Phillipson, 1998).

There are important implications here for how western society and the arrangement of political and economic structures create and sanction crime control policies grounded in such knowledge bases (Powell, 2001). Such knowledge bases are focused on: one, 'biological aging' which refers to the internal and external physiological changes that take place in the individual body: and the second, psychological aging which is understood as the developmental changes in mental functioning – the emotional and cognitive capacities. Scientific theories of aging can be distinguished from the social construction of aging: the first, focused on the bio-psychological or pathological constituent of aging: and the second, on how aging has been socially constructed.

Scientific models of aging have also been prone to what Harry R. Moody (1998) refers to as an "amalgam of advocacy and science" (quoted in Powell, 2001, 119) in a neo-liberal attempt to position individualized perceptions of aging under the guise of science and its perceived tenets of value-freedom, objectivity and precision (Biggs, 1993). However, a fundamental question is how science has stabilized itself within a positivist criminological discourse that reflects not history but the total preoccupation of science and the 'problems' of aging. The elderly population should be a source of concern if only because it is a growing population and if we are fortunate enough not to die young we will all become members of an aging population. The United Nations estimates that by the year 2025, the global population of those over 60 years will double, from 542 million in 1995 to around 1.2 billion people (Krug, 2002:125).

An aging population

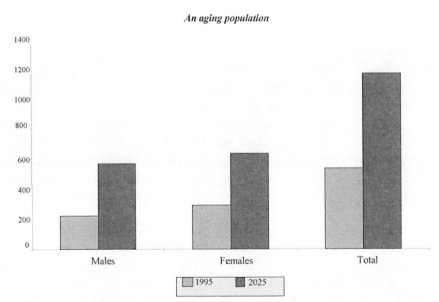

Source: United Nations Population Division, 2002 (in millions).

The term 'elderly' has been broadly applied by government departments to those aged 50 and over although societal assumptions and many researchers would tend towards retirement (another contested term) as a marker for the onset of 'old age' (Chivite-Matthews and Maggs 2002). The recent analysis of sexual violence reported to the British Crime Survey had a limited age range (See also Mirrlees-Black & Allen, 1998, Mirrlees et al 1998). The authors explain this as:

> "Although the BCS includes respondents aged 16 and over, the questions on inter-personal violence were only asked of those aged between 16 and 59. This was for two main reasons. First, older people have greater difficulty with or resistance to using a computer in this way … Secondly, it was thought that issues of elder abuse (from family members other than intimates) might get confused with responses about violence from intimates and that these issues were more appropriately dealt with in a specialized survey." (Walby and Allen 2004:118)

MAPPING OUT TERRAIN: THEORY, RESEARCH AND POLICY

The criminological relevance of age is rooted in the early post-war years with the concern about the consequences of demographic change and the potential shortage of 'younger' workers in western economies. Indeed, a significant contribution of social theories of criminology has been to highlight how individual lives and behavior which were thought to be determined solely by biological, medical and psychological factors, are, in fact, heavily influenced by *social environments* in which people live. Not only was age regarded as less important than race, class and gender but the dominant explanatory framework concerning aging came, as we discussed earlier with the notion of 'victim', from outside of social construction perspectives: scientific model. So it is of central importance that age came to be looked at in *social* terms.

Indeed, social researchers such as Gubrium (1974), quoting survey data collected in the late 1960s, suggest that older people are more often the victims of various kinds of fraud and elder abuse than younger people (although elder abuse, is not considered here as such, and is certainly underreported (Mawby and Walklate 1994)). One has to raise the question as to why elder abuse is rarely viewed as criminal (either in legal or consensual terms or as an object of criminological interest) in the same way as, for example, mugging.

Ageist discourse constructs and posits the elderly person in a dependency model (Phillipson & Biggs 1999). A pamphlet published in the UK by the charity Age Concern (1980), as part of its Action Against Crime Campaign states:

> 'Too many elderly people are worried. They have heard so much about crime and violence that they have become fearful, and worry reduces the quality of their lives' (p.3).

While older people would certainly benefit from more accurate information about the risk of vicitmization than they commonly receive through the mass media, their fear is related to the seriousness of the consequences if they were to be victimized, as well to the degree of the risk they face (See Mawby and Gill 1987, Skogan, 1987). When victimization occurs, it often happens in the person's own home, which is perceived as a serious violation of privacy and feelings of safety and tends to highlight people's feelings of dependency and vulnerability (Elias, 1986, Jones 1987).

For many reasons, the elderly population is a source of concern to social planners and to combat the fear of crime for the elderly age-homogenous living arrangements have been considered. Walker (1985) argues that the demographic situation for 'the population aged 65 and over is set to increase steadily (by one fifth overall) between 1983 and 2021. However, the largest increases are those aged 75 and over and 85 and over: 30 percent and 98 percent respectively. By the end of this period, women will outnumber men in the 85 and over age group by around 2.5 to 1' (Walker 1985:4). The 75 year-old and over group is the most vulnerable group within the elderly population. As Walker indicates (1985:6), 'there is a rapid increase in severe incapacity beyond the age of 70', in addition to which the elderly person is more likely to be living alone and to be housebound. This person is, typically, a physically frail widow. For such a person, who may be in a socially isolated position with diminishing, or limited financial resources, 'expressed feelings of crime or insecurity appear to have many sources, and to be strongly influenced by beliefs, attitudes and experiences which have nothing whatever to do with crime' (Sparks, Glenn and Dodd, 1977, p209). Those older people who have been victimized once tend to fear repeated offenses rather more than younger victims do. Older victims are less likely than crime victims in general to know 'their offender' or to be victimized outside the home (Fattah, 1993, Fattah and Sacco 1989; Mawby 1988) and such information can be used in the prevention of further victimization.

If older people are characterised by an overall low degree of victimization, then why have they been singled out as a specific group in research into the impact of crime? One possible answer can be found in the finding that, irrespective of age, those more concerned with the problem of crime and expressing the most fear of crime are not necessarily the most likely to experience victimization (Thomas and Hyman 1977).

We argue that 'age' is under-theorized and deemed unproblematic in the study of offenders and victims. We will demonstrate how 'age' is socially constructed, is represented, and the implications this has upon victimology and criminology. We will begin with an exploration of the development of victimology by looking at the early debates about victims that stem from the work of von Hentig (1948) and Mendelsohn (1947).

Fear of the possibility of being criminally victimized has become part of the discourse of the risk society we inhabit. We are haunted by the possibility that we could be the latest victim of a crime.

This ranges from the thought that a stranger could attack at any moment, either on the street or at home, and rob, assault, to, in the case of female victims, fear of rape. Although it must be noted that there are increasing reports of male-victim rapes (Home Office 1991), fear and the notion of vulnerability remain gendered (Dobash and Dobash, 1992, 2004). We see responses to fear of crime in the array of anti-theft devices; from CCTV cameras (Hughes,1991; Coleman, 2004) to 'gated communities' (Hughes, 1991) and other forms of institutional segregation and it is "through such expert systems of power-knowledge that the lives of older people have been regulated, ordered, known, and disciplined" (Twigg 2004:65). The fear of crime operates on a myriad of emotional and practical levels, from feeling vulnerable and isolated, to affecting one's personal well-being. As Moore and Trajanowitcz argue:

> 'Fear motivates people to invest and tie money in defensive measures to reduce their vulnerability. They stay indoors more than they would wish, avoid certain places, buy extra locks…' (Moore and Trajanowicz 1988:4).

Since the 1960s, fear of crime has been one of the major growth areas for both academic research and policy initiatives (Fattah, 1995). Perhaps inevitably, the major output on both fronts has been from criminologists and criminal justice system professionals in the U.S.A., but there has also been a growing international literature concerned with fear of crime and with measures to combat it. In the last 40 years, over 400 articles, conference papers, monographs and books have been written on some aspect or another on the fear of crime (See Hale 1996).

Thinking Critically About (missing text?)

A considerable amount of research has already identified a number of factors which appear to make a contribution to fear. Hale argues (1996) that these can be classified under the following headings:

1) Vulnerability
2) Environmental clues and conditions
3) Personal knowledge of crime and victimization
4) Confidence in the police and criminal justice systems
5) Perceptions of personal risk and
6) Seriousness of various offenses.

Many citizens may feel vulnerable for a number of reasons. Some may feel unable to protect themselves physically or economically (Pantazis, 2000), or be incapable of making a fast retreat, others may feel less able to cope with the physical and emotional consequences of being victimized (Toseland, 1982). Research has identified 4 groups who fall into this vulnerability category: the old (Antunes et al, 1977; Baldassare, 1986; Braungart et al, 1980; Clarke and Lewis, 1982; Giles-Sims, 1984; Yin 1985), women (Gordon et al, 1980; Warr 1985), the poor and ethnic minorities (Taylor and Hale 1986, Box et al 1986, 1988). Three environmental clues – incivilities, neighborhood housing conditions, and neighborhood cohesion all make a contribution towards fear of crime, particularly for elderly people.

We suggested earlier that ageist constructions underlie the common assumptions that older people are particularly 'vulnerable' to the negative effects of crime and fear. With regard to financial victimization, it is widely acknowledged that the legal framework relating to handling other people's money is extremely complex but lacks safeguards for vulnerable older people (Powell, 2001).

As with other characteristics which make older people vulnerable to victimization, it is difficult to disentangle the age factor from other variables which means that older people figure prominently among those for whom victimization has a high impact. In terms of actual rates of victimization, older people are at relatively low risk from crime (although elder abuse, which is not considered here as such, is certainly underreported) (Mawby and Walklate 1994).

Certainly, the analysis between of the relationship between older people, victimization and the criminal justice system (See Brogden and Nighar, 2000) challenges the stereotype that the elderly are a homogeneous, vulnerable social group. Many citizens across the life-course may feel vulnerable for a number of reasons. As this chapter demonstrates, what has been constructed as a 'problem' for elders i.e. being potential victims of crime, for the majority may not be a problem. Where the elderly are identified as the most vulnerable in our communities is in respect of abuse of people who are dependent upon their assailant for essential daily care and vulnerable to fraud (See Bennett et al 1997). Older victims tend to report that crime has a high and long-lasting impact upon them compared to younger victims (Skogan, 1987).

Pain succinctly argues:

> 'The structures of class, gender, race and ability are the key determinants of how older people experience old age. It is these which underpin where older people live, their socio-economic status and their risk of victimization, whether from property crime, harassment in the community or abuse by carers within domestic spheres' (Pain 2003:62).

The reason for low victimization rates among the elderly are that women and older people avoid going out at night because they do not feel safe doing so. Fattah and Sacco (1989) conclude in their study of crime against older people in North America that:

> 'While it may be fashionable to view the fear of crime as an irrational response on the part of elderly to a world that does not truly threaten them, such a conceptualization is probably not appropriate. Rather than irrationality, elderly fear of crime may represent the exercise of caution by a group in society that frequently lacks the control necessary to manage the risk of criminal harm or to marshal the resources necessary to offset its consequences' (226)

While they may be relatively unlikely to become victims of crime, their fears are understandable: if they are poor, in poor health, isolated, house bound and if they feel vulnerable, their ability to withstand victimization may be substantially reduced. As Powell (2001) explains, the level of feeling unsafe among older people was conditional upon their level of deprivation and multiple deprivations increase fear levels. The combined determinants of gender, poverty and age result in potentially higher rates of fear and vulnerability amongst elderly women than in other social groups. Older people are more fearful of crime than other groups within society. More research is required to identify the inter-relationships between age, neighborhood, poverty and fear of crime and its contribution to social exclusion of older people.

Reflection

This paper has explored 'age' as an important dimension of analysis. We have dissected its relationship to victimization and contemporary criminology by focusing on particular representations and experiences of older people. We have traced the historiography of the concept of "victim" and contextualized the competing theories of victimology: science versus social constructionism. We have highlighted how in its original 'scientific' form, victimology examined the pathological characteristics of victims and how they "contributed" to their own victimization. As a counter to this, we traced the emergence of social construction of victimization which looks to how society impacts on and shapes the construction of victimization.

We have explored the relationship between the scarce sociological study of old age and victimization and highlighted a number of implications for the study of age and its relationship to 'vulnerability'.

Finally, we suggest that the marginalization of older people adds to hegemonic criminal justice practices leading to injustice, oppression and marginalization in contemporary society. In order to prevent marginalization and multiple victimization, it is crucial to examine the role of victimological 'dominant assumptions' (Pain 1997), criminal justice policy and social practices. A fusion of theoretical inquiry and active participation of older people and victims in victim policy process and victimological research would address pervasive cultural values central to the empowerment-marginalization nexus based on 'age' and 'victimization'.

So how can the relationship between later life, crime and victimology be addressed? In our discussion we have examined how and why age and ageist discourses are deployed in the study of crime and later life. As the reader, you may ask why the older victim is presented by media reports, government policy and in some research as the archetypal victim. Secondly, you may ask why criminologists, victimologists and government policy advisors have produced a wealth of literature on young persons and offenders but have neglected problematizing age. One possible reason for the neglect of later life issues in all of the above is that youth as with the study of offenders unleashes the voyeur and allows us to reminisce about our own youth styles. In contrast, the study of old age and crime as Pollak (1941), astutely observed approximately 60 years ago, evokes a different reaction:

> 'Old criminals offer an ugly picture and it seems as if even scientists do not like to look at it for any considerable amount of time.....On the other hand, if the thesis of the inter-relationship between age and crime is to hold, an investigation of all its implications has to yield results, and with the tendency of our population to increase in the higher age brackets, a special study of criminality of the aged is required' (1941:212).

If Pollak's view was accurate in 1941, it is even more so today, over sixty years later. With the elder prison population representing the fastest growing age group in our prison system, we have reached an important juncture in the disciplines of gerontology and criminology.

Women and men in later life need improved health services, different types of housing, age-sensitive regimes, and a variety of aids when they become disabled. We have to recognize that the elderly inmate, due to the effects of aging, has far different needs and places far different demands on a system that is designed for the younger inmate. But they also need a reason for using these things. 'In our society, the purpose of life in old age is often unclear...Old age is seen as a 'problem' with the elderly viewed as dependants; worse still, they are often described as a non-productive burden upon the economy' (Phillipson, 1982:166). Hence, it is not surprising that elders experience isolation and alienation when they are denied access to the sources of meaning valued by the society in which they live (Phillipson & Walker, 1986; Turner, 1988).

SUMMARY AND CONCLUSIONS

For many years, both gerontologists and criminologists have concentrated their attention exclusively in their respective fields (Malinchak, 1980). In this chapter, we have synergized criminological and gerontological theories to understand and problematize the complexity of aging, victimization and crime and, in turn, place the needs of elders firmly on the research and policy agenda.

The evidence presented here demonstrates that although older people are portrayed as victims of crime, statistically they are least likely to be and the actuality of being a victim of crime in this respect is inversely disproportionate to the fear of crime. However, one must stress that the experience of *fear* is very real to the individual and thus makes measuring degrees of fear impossible (Box et al 1988). Sparks (1992) rhetorically asks, 'What is a rational level of fear? In other words, we argue, that if *fear* is *experienced* then ultimately; it is *real*'.

The consequences of Sparks' (1992) question are immense: there is the creation of what Estes, Biggs and Phillipson (2004) describe as 'No Care Zones', where victim support may disintegrate in the face of inadequate services and benefits for older people. On the other side, there may equally be the emergence of 'No Identity Zones', these reflecting the absence of spaces in which to construct a viable identity for later-life compared to other age groups (Phillipson and Biggs 1999).

Traditionally, questions concerning discrimination in criminal processing have focused on the effects of factors such as gender, ethnicity, disability, sexuality, socio-economic status and age (for those between 10–18), but have neglected later-life issues (See Chapter 3). Their experiences have remained marginalized in the debates around policy, and how the criminal justice system responds to these changes remains yet to be seen. By theorizing age, victimization and crime, we hope to dispel and challenge some of the myths surrounding later-life, crime and the older victim.

Chapter 2

AGING, CRIME AND PRISONS

INTRODUCTION

Since the 1980s, prison officials, policymakers, and researchers have witnessed an astonishing phenomenon in the US, UK, Japan and Germany: increasing numbers of older adults are entering the criminal justice system and in particular, prison: finding themselves locked behind steel doors and razor wire fences. So much so that researchers and policymakers are beginning to turn their attention to examine policy issues such as economic costs, housing, end-of-life issues and institutional management of older offenders. This chapter explores this neglected yet increasingly important topic of older offenders. Older people have been stereotyped as 'harmless', 'vulnerable', and 'victims of crime', however, less is known about older people who are criminal offenders. While it may be true that older adults are more often victims of crime than being actual offenders, it is also true that older people commit crime, some as career criminals, but many others as first time offenders. Since older people are known to be victims of crime rather than offenders there is a very sparse body of literature that captures what is known about older adults as criminal offenders and the experiences of those incarcerated. Unfortunately, the picture is not coherent. The purpose of this chapter is to sociologically examine what is known about older adults as offenders. This will be accomplished through examining the types of crime committed by older people and the risk factors associated with the commitment of crime among elder offenders. It is important that older offenders are accurately portrayed because not only will it dispel and challenge the myths about older offenders but it will also look to providing a comparative analysis in highlighting commonalities and differences in managing the needs of older offenders.

Academic understanding of 'age' and offending has been focused around younger people's experiences to the exclusion of older people. Although young people have long been associated with crime, it appears that, as is the case with social class, different age groups commit different types of crime. Many theories deal almost exclusively with juvenile delinquency. Hence, it has been stated that 'one of the few facts agreed on in criminology is the age distribution of crime' (Hirschi and Gottfredson, 1983:552). A series of moral panics have, 'demonized young people, from the teddy boys, mods and rockers of the 1960s, through to punks, skinheads, muggers, joyriders girl gangs and mobile phone snatchers of 2000 (see for example, Cohen, 1973; Pearson, 1983; Curtis, 1999). As this chapter will show, the assumption that crime is overwhelmingly a 'young person's game' must be called into question. As criminology has developed, similar to the trajectory of gerontology, it has moved from a discipline embedded in scientific positivism to one in which diverse theories have enriched an understanding of social construction and experiences of crime. It is interesting that the concept of age as understood in Criminology has not provided a full explanation of its social construction of age as it has omitted an understanding of a more rounded conceptualization of age because of both its institutional over-emphasis on younger people and under-emphasis on older people. Yet, the study of crime and *aging* has omitted the experiences of older people. It has only been recently that this has been taken seriously as a focus of concern relating to aging and crime (Wahidin, 2004).

What is both important and critical about aging, then, is how a society uses it to socially construct people into 'categories'. As a classificatory tool, age is important in three ways. First, like sex, age is an ascribed status or characteristic, which is, based on attributes over which we have little or no control. Second, unlike sex, a specific age is always transitional – constantly moving from one age to another, beginning life at zero and ending with a certain 'number' at death that is regulated by societal expectations of age-appropriate behavior. These transitions also assume that conformity is rewarded whereas deviance is punished. The unique aspect of aging is that everyone can expect to occupy various positions throughout life on the basis of his or her age.

At any point of a lifespan, age simultaneously denotes a set of social constructs, defined by the norms specific to a given society at a specific point in history. Thus, a specific period of life: infancy, childhood, adolescence, adulthood, middle age or old age is influenced by the structural entities of a given society. Therefore, aging is not to be considered the mere product of biological-psychological function rather a consequence of socio-cultural factors and subsequent life-chances. Historically, the stages of life were presented as a religious discourse, which formed the basis for the cultural expectations about behavior and appearance across the life-course. The life stage model is still taken for granted and popularly used in society which impinges on how our lives are structured albeit by bio-medical discourses of 'decline'.

'Old age' throughout the past two hundred years has been seen as a social and medical "problem" and this predominant perspective is evident through the language used by policymakers, mass media and the general public. A significant contribution of criminology as a discipline has been to highlight how individual lives and behavior which were thought to be determined solely by biological, medical and psychological factors, are, in fact, heavily influenced and constrained by social environments in which individuals live. However, it is quite astonishing that given the range and explosion of such sociological ideas that there was not, until recently, much consideration and application of such critical criminological ideas to 'aging'. This chapter addresses such conceptual and empirical deficits by exploring three main areas: one, the importance of gerontological theory in the construction of aging; two, by expanding the criminological disciplinary base by incorporating an understanding of aging; finally, we then move our analysis to explore the concept of aging to address an increasingly important criminological topic: the experiences of older offenders in the criminal justice system with particular reference to the prison systems in England and Wales, the United States, Germany and Japan.

The next section starts to look more specifically at the problems and limitations that older people as prisoners have had in the US, UK, Germany and Japan. A comparative assessment illustrates the growing 'aging prison population' that has implications for the experiences of older prisoners.

AGING AND IMPRISONMENT: COMPARATIVE TRENDS – AMERICA, UK, GERMANY AND JAPAN

Much of the global debate on older offenders is over how to define 'old' (Phillips, 2005). The first problem arises with the definition of 'elderly', 'elder' or 'older', which can produce information that at first appears contradictory. Official statistics on the age breakdown of offenses and prison statistics (see Home Office, 1997a, 1997b) use anything between 21 and 59 or simply give figures for offenders aged 21 and above. Some previous researchers have defined older prisoners as those 65 years of age and older (Newman, 1984), some 60 (Kratcoski, 1990) and 55 (Goetting, 1992). However, the majority of studies such as Phillips (1996), Wahidin (2002), Aday (2003), the American Department of Justice and units for older prisoners in the UK have used 50-55 as the threshold age to define when one becomes an older offender. This definition is supported by the fact that offenders experience what is known as 'accelerated' aging, so that a typical prisoner in their 50s has the physical appearance and accompanying health problems of someone at least ten years older in the outside community. As the Health Care Manager at one UK male prison in the North West of England, Her Majesty's Prison Wymott states, "in the prison service you find people presenting health problems that are normally found in the over 65s at a much younger age". For the purpose of this chapter, the term 'older' or 'offender in later life' or 'elder' will be used interchangeably to denote a person aged fifty or over.

There has been surprisingly little research undertaken on older offenders – certainly when compared with the amount of attention paid by criminologists to similar prisoner cohorts. Research by Aday (1979), Phillips (1996) and more recently by Wahidin (2004) has begun to correct this. However, the literature available on elder offenders is still restricted to predominantly American - based research (Aday, 1995, Anderson et al 1989, Newman et al, 1984). The literature suggests that it was in the USA, in the 1980s, that the issue of the so-called 'white-haired offender' first became a subject of interest locating the elderly offender in a medical and welfarist model (Aday and Webster, 1979; Aday, 1994a; Schichor, 1984). However, Gewerth (1988) argues that 'the problem of crime amongst the aged may be newly recognized, but it is certainly not new. Research interest in criminal behavior among the elderly dates back to the early part of the century – the phenomenon was first discussed at a criminology conference in Budapest in 1899' (Pollack, 1941:213 cited in Gewerth 1988:15; Cullen, Wozniak and Frank, 1985).The work of Aday (1979,1994a, 1994b) has been ground-breaking in the writing of the elderly male offender in the United States and more recently, on his work on older female offenders in 2007 (Aday, Farney, Wahidin, 2007).

THE GREYING OF THE AMERICAN PRISON POPULATION

The latest figures show that on December 31, 2006, – 2,258,983 prisoners were held in Federal or State prisons or in local jails. With nearly 500,000 people age 50 and above incarcerated each year in America, corrections officials are facing the problem of what to do with the aging prison population. The greying of American's prisons became particularly noticeable during the 1990s as the number of prisoners 50 years of age and older in federal and state institutions more than tripled (33, 499 in 1990 to more than 125,000 in 2002 (*Corrections Yearbook*, 2003)). In 2002, the 50 and older population comprised 8.2 % of the total prison population---nearly double the 4.9 % statistic of 1990. To further illustrate the exponential growth of this subgroup of prisoners, older men and women comprise over 10 % of the total prison population in 19 states, a growth from 7 states in 1990. Lifers and prisoners with 20-plus year sentences now constitute one-quarter of the total inmate population (*Corrections Yearbook*, 2003). Women only constitute a small percentage (5%) of the older prison population, but their numbers are growing rapidly (American Correctional Association, 2003). Just under 50 % of older prisoners are in federal and state prisons in the United States and are first time offenders (primarily murder and sex crimes) against relatives or close acquaintances aged 50 plus (Beck, 1997).

As previous research has shown, aging prisoners are a diverse population (Aday, 1994; Douglass 1991; Kerbs 2000). Most older prisoners in the States are unmarried, are male (95%) and have fewer than twelve years of formal education. With the exception of Southern states, where older black prisoners outnumber their white counterparts. The mean age of older prisoners in the United States is 57. A significant number were either unemployed or working in unskilled labor at the time of offense, had no access to preventative health care, and thus now, as in the UK, the prison service is finding that older people's health needs in prison are more resource intensive than any other group. It is estimated based on a study in the United States that healthcare and security for prisoners over the age of 60 typically cost in the region of $70,000 (Shimkus 2004). That is three times as much as for younger prisoners.

Research conducted in several States (Aday, 1995; Aday 2001; Colsher, Wallace et al 1992) has found that older male prisoners frequently suffer from a variety of chronic health problems. The most common age related illnesses are: arthritis, hypertension, heart problems and emphysema. As a whole, they have a higher incidence of chronic disease and significant functional disability compared to similar age groups on the outside (Edwards, 1998).

The 1976 *Estelle vs Gamble* ruling stated that prisoners have an obligation to provide for the medical and personal needs of all prisoners including the 2,500 dying behind bars every year (Byock, 2002). Compassionate release from prison is considered an important alternative to prison hospice care. While laws vary from state to state, 43 states have reported the availability of compassionate release (Anno et al. 2004). For example, when the State of Virginia abolished parole in 1994, it also created a possible loophole for older prisoners. Prisoners aged 60 or older who have served at least 10 years of their sentence, or those 65 and older who have been incarcerated for at least 5 years are allowed to petition the parole board for geriatric release. Ten years later, not a single geriatric prisoner has received an early release (Hammack 2004). Moreover, America's courts do not mandate prisons to release terminally ill, older or infirm prisoners, but some federal and state prisons do provide compassionate release for prisoners who have medical records and physicians statements documenting their prognoses. Sending minimal risk, terminally ill prisoners home to die reduces prison medical expenditures (Yates and Gillespie 2000), but placing prisoners in the care of others is not always possible. For example, the Texas Criminal Justice Department reported that two elderly prisoners in their 70s suffering from chromic heart and lung failure required around the clock intensive medical care that is costing taxpayers nearly $1 million a month (Montiz 2004). Prison officials cannot release the two men to a nursing home where their medical bills would be lower because Texas law forbids the early release of those convicted of sex crimes. In many cases, aging relatives often do not have the strength, stamina or time adequate to support a frail elderly prisoner, and nursing staff are generally reluctant to assume the liability of caring for former prisoners (Aday, 2003). Therefore, prison officials must provide in-house health services and treatment programs for prisoners who have no other option but to spend their remaining days behind bars.

In the UK, contrary to popular belief, statistics from the Home Office (2008) show that the most common offenses for the older female age group are not perpetrated by the menopausal shoplifter (see Wahidin 2005a); they are not theft and handling or fraud and forgery, but violence against the person and drug offenses. By comparison, the most common offenses for men in this group are sexual offenses, violence against a person, and drug offenses which is similar to the general prison population (MoJ, population in custody, England and Wales, October 2007).

Women in prison of all ages form only a very small proportion of the total prison population although the number of women in prison has more than doubled over the past decade. On the 30th June 2007, the total prison population for England and Wales was 81,040. The women's prison population in England and Wales stood at 4,390 which represents 5% of the total prison population and women over 50 represent only 7% of the total female prison estate and in terms of actual figures there were 294 women over the age of 50.

Men in prison in England and Wales constitute 94% of the total prison population and on the 30 June 2007, the total male prison population was 76,299. More than one in ten male older prisoners who are over 60 belong to a minority ethnic group, which is three times higher than the proportion of the general population[5]. For the same period, men over 50 represent 9% of the male estate and in terms of actual numbers, there were *6,524. The greatest percentage growth in the prison population based on age is for men who are 80+ and for women it is in 70-79 age range.*

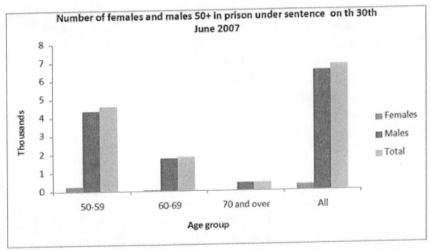

Source: Figures adapted Wahidin 2008.

Information regarding the older prison population in Germany is still in its infancy and on March 31st, 2006, there were 6,755 people who were 50+ above serving a prison sentence or kept in preventive detention (Personal communication: AW with Professor Goergen, Head of the German Police

---

[5] Prison Reform Trust (2003), Growing Old in Prison, London: Prison Reform Trust.

Academy: 4/4/08) and in 2003, there were 955 over 60 years old (Times: 16/11/04). The number of older women on March 31st 2008 was 429 (Personal communication: AW with Professor Goergen, Head of the German Police Academy: 4/4/08). Germany is now beginning to address the growing crisis by creating a specialist facility for older men in the State of Lower Saxony which has wheelchair access, hospital-style beds, close to the local hospital and provides hospice care similar to that found at Louisiana State Penitentiary: Angola Prison. At the Oregon Department of Corrections geriatric unit (Anno et al, 2004), prisoners are provided with hoists, toilets, showers that comply with the American Disability Act of 1990 (ADA), and older prisoners also have a therapeutic gym equipped with a pool-table configured at a lower height to accommodate wheel chairs. Close-captioned television and specially equipped phones are available for the hearing impaired. According to prison officials in the Oregon Department of Corrections, expenditure is significantly reduced when housing older offenders in an environment where specially trained health care staff can recognize and treat problems before they become severe. In 51 states, provisions are made for older prisoners ranging from: being grouped or placed in geriatric facilities; having access to specific tailored programs for the older offender, chronic care clinics on site; hospice/end-of-life programs (Mezey, Dubler, Mitty and Bordy, 2002) and in the following states listed including Alabama, Georgia, Florida, Oklahoma, Wisconsin, Illinois, Kentucky, West Virginia, Virginia, Tennessee, Louisiana, Pennsylvania, Mississippi, North Carolina , Texas, Ohio, Wisconsin, and New Mexico, stand-alone facilities or secure nursing homes have been established to accommodate the increasing number of older prisoners (See Aday, 1999, 2006; American Correctional Association, 2004, Neffe 1997). The model of the older prison in Lower Saxony is based on the Onichimi prison in Japan.

In comparison to the above, Japan, which is one of the world's most rapidly aging societies, is confronting a sharp increase in the number of older criminals and prisoners. In 2003, 30,000 Japanese aged over 65 were arrested and the number of elderly suspects has risen by 320% in the past decade (Times: 16/11/04). From 2000 to 2006, the number of older prisoners soared by 160 percent, to 46,637, from 17,942, according to Japan's National Police Agency. Shoplifting accounted for 54 percent of the total in 2006 and petty theft for 23%. While the main reason behind the explosion in greying lawbreakers is the rapid aging of Japan's population, the rates have far outpaced the increase of older people in the general population. Between 2000 and 2006, while the total population of Japanese 60 and over rose by 17%, prisoners of the same age group swelled by 87%. In the country's 74 prisons, the proportion of older prison rose to 12.3% in 2006 from 9.3% in 2000, while the share of those in their 20s declined and in other age groups remained flat. Japan's rates are much higher than those in the West.

Researchers at the University of Fukushima say that prison is seen as an attractive option for retirement, 'compared with run down council housing estates with broken lifts'. The 65 and over group now make up the fastest-growing group of offenders and in contrast to the UK and the US, the rise is being driven by mostly non-violent crime.

AN EMPIRICAL EXAMPLE OF OLDER OFFENDERS AND IMPRISONMENT: THE CASE OF THE UK AND US

The empirical base of this section of the chapter draws on data from Wahidin's work in the area of older offenders in the criminal justice system of England and Wales and the work of Aday, Farney, Wahidin (2007) in the US. This highlights an important case study by focusing on comparative analysis of older offenders in the UK and the US.

This next section of the chapter involves interviewed prison officers, healthcare managers, governors, men and women in later-life serving a period of imprisonment (see Wahidin, 2005b, Aday et al, 2007). At the time of the interviews, all of the eligible women and men who were on the prison roll consented to participate in the research (Wahidin, 2002, 2004, Aday et al 2007). This was possible mainly because the women and the men themselves approved of the study and had accepted it as relevant to their experiences. For the above studies with prisoners, participation was encouraged through the prison grapevine. The shipping of prisoners to other prisons assisted in facilitating the research process[4]. The sample consisted of the following categories of prisoner:

---

[4] 'Shipped out' is a colloquial prison term also known as 'being ghosted' and means being taken to another prison often without warning and in some cases by force. It is used as a disciplinary measure. It can also mean that the prisoner is moved because she or he has requested a transfer. The actual process of moving prisoners in this way is highly problematic for critical criminologists. This movement of prisoners (for the reasons stated above) could facilitate another meeting with the woman in a different prison whereupon she would encourage others to participate in the research. This happened on several occasions.

1) The first-time offender currently serving a term of imprisonment;
2) The offender who has had previous convictions but not served a prison sentence before;
3) The offender who has previously served a custodial term after conviction;
4) Prisoners serving a life sentence and who have simply grown old in prison;
5) Long term prisoners.

When thinking about older people as perpetrators of crime we associate them with relatively minor offenses such as shoplifting, fraud or driving under the influence of alcohol. However, there have been recent exceptions in the UK with high profile cases such as Harold Shipman, Rosemary West and the general rise in the number of men who have been convicted in later-life for sex-related offenses, including those charged with 'historical offenses' (offenses committed two/three decades ago). The majority of men in prison aged 60 and over (56%) have committed sex offenses (PRT 2007). Criminology has, until recently, ignored later-life and crime-related activities, and Pain (1997), suggests that the reason for this is that old age:

"… has largely been overlooked by criminologists, the debate so far being located mainly in medical and social welfare disciplines" (1997, 18).

Moreover, this silence and exclusion around elders in prison on the part of policymakers and criminologists is a reflection of the ageist society we inhabit. For example, the Governor at Her Majesty's Prison (HMP) Kingston, which was first unit in England and Wales in 2005 to create a specialist facility for the older male prison, argues that the closure of the 'Elderly Unit' was led by a policy directive not to make sufficient funds available to sustain the unit. Thus, the closure was due to "not being able to do what we really wanted to do, with people of this age, and that really was the straw that broke the camel's back. The lows were having to say we would love to do more but we can't because of the lack of resources. At the moment, there is no real political imperative to do anything about older prisoners. I did take the prison minister round. He sat on the bed of a dying prisoner. I thought that might make a difference. To be honest - it is *out of sight and out of mind,* because *nobody really wants to know*".

It is evident from Her Majesty's Chief Inspectorate report on prisons (2004), 'Not Old and Quiet: Older Offenders in Prison', and from the above statistics that indeed the older prison population is becoming one of the fastest growing groups in England Wales without any comprehensive policy or strategy in place to address their needs.

The largest concentration of male prisoners aged 50+ in 2003 was at HMP Kingston. Subsequent to its closure in May 2005, HMP Norwich L Wing, HMP Frankland B Wing and HMP Wymott I Wing (the Elderly and Disabled Community) replaced the function of the Elderly Unit at HMP Kingston. Although HMP Holloway and HMP New Hall are both closed prisons and have the highest percentage of women in the 50+ category, they have ano facilities or formal policies in place to address their specific needs. As numbers are predicted to increase (as a result of bifurcation, indeterminate sentences in sentencing), this group will surely pose particular challenges to the current physical environment, healthcare facilities and regime. Moreover, the quality of treatment in the prison setting for this cohort has fallen short of the acceptable standards outlined by the Human Rights Act of 1998 (implemented in October 2000) and the Disability Discrimination Act 2005. The Department of Health is currently developing a health policy for older prisoners and the Disability Discrimination Act (2005) now applies to prison[6]. This means that the prison service has to take reasonable steps to ensure that prisoners with disabilities can access facilities in prison. However, there is little evidence so far of the prison service is responding to this directive. It is evident from the literature and Her Majesty' Chief Inspector's Thematic Review (2004) that prisons in general are failing to deal with this particular group's specific needs, although there are pockets of excellence: such as HMP Norwich – L Wing, HMP Wymott I Wing and HMP Frankland B Wing (see Wahidin 2005b). These units or wings provide tailored programs and activities, and the environment is less brutal and more sanitized than in the normal prison location. The cacophony of prison noise is reduced, cell doors have been widened to accommodate wheel chairs, hoists are in place, nurses and occupational therapists are available to bathe those who are infirm, and experts are brought in to liaise with the prison to find effective strategies to address and manage the health, social and care needs of this age group.

The older units discussed have developed at a local level through the work of dedicated officers, governors and health teams, who have identified the

---

[6] Personal communication between AW and the Department of Health.(change # of superscript here and above to 5)

health, welfare and social care needs of offenders in later-life. The governor at HMP Kingston explains that the Elderly Unit at Kingston evolved purely because "Kingston had a number of older lifers / life sentence prisoners at the time the idea for an older unit was discussed. We also had some available space to do something. A number of staff said, "why don't we try and create a different environment for older prisoners away from the hustle and bustle of the main prison?" So the unit happened almost by default because there were already some older guys here". Aday et al (2006) in their study based at various state penitentiaries in the United States and the work of Wahidin (2006) revealed similarities of concern for the prisoners were as follows:

1) Loss of health, freedom, and privacy.
2) Relationships with friends and family members, other inmates, and prison staff and guards.
3) Coping strategies such as religion, rehabilitation, and prison friendships.
4) End-of-life issues.

Of all the issues and concerns that surfaced from the interviews, three central themes emerged: family concerns, health and healthcare concerns, and hopes and fears for the future.

The American criminal justice system has been at the forefront of delivering special programs for older offenders (Krajick, 1979; Aday and Rosenfield, 1992). In this sense, 'special programs' constitute the distinctive treatment of the elderly prisoner housed in an age-segregated or in an age-sensitive environment. Segregation provides a concentration of specialized staff and resources for the elderly, thereby reducing costs (Florida Corrections Commission 2001).

Previous research supports the notion that participation in a specific group increases self-respect and increases the capability to resume community life once released. A choice of age-segregation or age-integration provides older prisoners with the opportunity of forming peer networks, while at the same time, reducing vulnerability and violence they may encounter in the mainstream of prison life. Fattah & Sacco state:

'Concern for their safety and the need to protect them against victimization, exploitation and harassment outweigh any stabilizing effect their integration may have' (1989:101).

It is imperative that the prison systems in the US, England Wales, Germany and Japan provide not only comprehensive opportunities while in prison and appropriate resettlement programs, but also alternatives to the traditional custodial framework in which elders find themselves growing old. What is needed is the flexibility of having accommodation and provision reserved for elders, without creating a separate prison or excluding elders from the main prison environment. Aday succinctly states: 'Like the elderly in the free world, they are familiar with life in the general population and perceive that it has a mark of independence' (2003:146). The criminal justice system in England and Wales, unlike the American criminal justice system, is still operating without a comprehensive plan to respond adequately to a pending crisis. The needs of elders in prisons are substantial, and can include physical, mental and preventative healthcare; custody classification to special housing, educational, vocational or recreational programs, physical exercise, and rehabilitation programming; dietary considerations and long-term geriatric and nursing care.

An overriding theme within the integration versus segregation debate is that the way forward is to provide flexible accommodation, not through segregation, but through integration, within a framework of tolerance, understanding and adaptability. The aging prison population poses a true dilemma, and deserves recognition both among those interested in the well-being of those in later-life and those executing prison policy. Age, in time, will be considered as one of the biggest issues that will continue to affect the criminal justice system and prison healthcare in the future. With the continued increase in criminal activity among the elderly population as a whole, learning more about crime and aging, and about institutional adjustment, recidivism and release, seems imperative.

'OUT OF SIGHT – OUT OF MIND': THE INVISIBLE MINORITY

Despite the discipline of criminology having a rich imagination, the experiences of older people and the criminal justice system have been excluded. In the 1980s, it was *de rigueur* not to start any paper on the topic of women and crime without reference to the dearth of material in this field and the general neglect of gender issues. Twenty years on, the impact of feminist criminology has opened up new areas of study and the broader point is that gender approaches and theories have enriched every aspect of the discipline. Similarly, as with the inclusion of feminist discourses in criminology, the incorporation of gerontology in examining older people in the criminal justice system will enrich the discipline so that the continual denial and discrimination of older people in prison can and will be challenged.

Without UK data on current healthcare expenditure, one has to turn to studies conducted in the US to understand the future resource implications of an older prison population. Several American and UK studies have indicated that older prisoners cost, on average, three times as much as a younger prisoner (Gallagher, 1990; Fazel et al 2001). At HMP Wymott, with a population of just under 700 men, 60% of all bed-watches were allocated to the prisoners over 50 who comprised 15% of the population (Wahidin 2005b). In comparison, despite making up only 8% of the total prison population in the US, prisoners over 50 were responsible for 19% of the costs paid for ambulatory surgery episodes; 17% of costs for non-emergency room episodes; 31% of costs for ancillary care episodes; 20% of costs for specialty care episodes; and 29% of costs for inpatient care episodes (Florida Corrections Commission, 2001). As long as these conditions remain in place, prison healthcare costs will continue to increase dramatically. A similar pattern is emerging in the prison system in England and Wales. The factors Aday, Krabil and Wahidin (2004) found influencing the increase in expenditure are the following:

1) The rising cost of health care in society at large;
2) The increasing number of prisoners in the prison system;
3) The general aging of the prison population;
4) The higher prevalence of infectious diseases among prison populations.

As long as these trends continue, prison healthcare costs will continue to increase. Like prisoners in general, aging prisoners have not had proper access to healthcare on the outside. They often come into the prison system with numerous chronic illnesses and consume multiple medications. Jonathan Turley, director of *Project for Older Prisoners* (POP'S), noted that: "the greatest single contributor to the high costs of older prisoners is medical expenditures" (Turley, 1990:26). On average, prisoners over the age of 50 suffer at least three chronic health problems, such as hypertension, diabetes and emphysema (Acoca, 1998; Turley, 1990). The most common illnesses were psychiatric, cardiovascular, musculoskeletal and respiratory (PRT 2003).

Prisoners, as a population, traditionally have medical and social histories that put them more at risk for illness and disease than those who haven't been incarcerated and over half of all older prisoners suffer from a mental disorder. As the number of older prisoners increases, the prison system will be even more challenged to provide adequate health and social care provision.

Imprisonment for many women and men in later-life answers the first part of the statement of purpose, i.e. "Her Majesty's Prison Service serves the public by keeping in custody those committed by the courts"[6]. The second part of the statement of purpose is answered by providing a milieu therapy.

Elders in prison have concerns regarding how they become and are marginalized, within a space which claims to enable women and men across the life-course to 'lead useful lives in custody and after release'. Their exclusion from the limited activities is a disabling practice, which makes them feel that they have no role to play. It enforces dependency and leads to institutionalization. An elder male prisoner succinctly states, that after 30 years of imprisonment, "I am institutionalized. I am afraid of the outside, because I have been in prison for over 30 years. The prison officers and the Governor virtually tell you what to do. They run your life. Well... people have been running my life, *all* my life. I was brought up in a home. Ever since I was 10 years old, people have said, 'you've got to do this'. 'You've got to do that'. 'You go to bed at this time and so it goes on'. So one becomes used to the idea of being told what to do. So suddenly, if it is withdrawn then you are like a fish out of water".

Prison, is a place *for* punishment rather than merely *as* punishment. The cumulative pains of imprisonment already described compound the feelings of estrangement and alienation from the outside world. They are, as Bauman argues, in an 'unseen place' (2000:103). But, as the extract below shows, prison doesn't have to *do* anything 'extra' to women in order to be *for* (and not just *as*) punishment – confinement and separation from their life context *per se* results in continual guilt and anxiety about the people they are responsible for. In this sense, prison *as* and prison *for* punishment are one and the same thing. This may be particularly severe for older women who have spent their lives coping with responsibilities for others and have built their self-esteem upon being competent and reliable carers and partners. For many, the experiences of imprisonment lead to a sense of helplessness: "you just feel that you are bound and gagged from head to toe and there is no escaping that situation. Prison, it's not just taking you out of society to say you've done this thing and you've got

---

[6] q.v.1

to be removed from society and be punished but the punishment just continues on. It starts from the day you are arrested and just continues on and on and on. But it's not just the punishment of being away from home. If only if it was that easy. *But it is the one hundred and one things that happen every day of the week. That is the punishment".*

The UK, unlike America, is still operating without a comprehensive plan to respond adequately to the growing numbers of older prisoners. Today we have family courts and a large variety of special courts to handle specific problems. Along with the medley of juridical experts from child psychiatrists to social workers, will we in the future see court reports and parole boards informed by gerontologists who can advise the proper referral service for elders caught in the criminal justice system? Will we see the development of 'an Older Offenders Justice Board' similar to the Youth Offending Board? Could we then be accused of infantilizing the older offender if we advocated a court which deals specifically with older offenders? Should we change our sentencing structure to reflect probable years remaining in the offender's life?[7] For example, a fifteen-year sentence for a sixty-five year old is practically a life sentence, while a twenty-five year old who spends fifteen years in prison still has a thirty-year life expectancy after s/he leaves prison. This practice condemns the older offender to spend a greater percentage of her or his remaining life in prison. This disparity could be reduced by giving older offenders sentences which represent the same percentage of their remaining lives as those given to younger persons. For example, the average twenty-five year-old male can expect to live for 46.9 more years. If such a person were convicted of a crime which carries a twenty-year prison term, he would spend approximately 43% of his remaining life behind bars. A sixty-five-year-old is expected to live 14.2 more years. A twenty-year sentence would thus represent 141% of this defendant's remaining life, a *de facto* life sentence. By contrast, 43% of his life would be only 6.1 years (see James 1992). In *State v. Waldrip,*[8] the judge reduced a sixty-seven year-old defendant's sentence for voluntary manslaughter from five years to life to five to ten years, recognizing that even the minimum term of five years could theoretically be a life sentence because of the defendant's age (ibid). It can be argued that if an older person does not

---

[7] Cristina Pertierra (1995) presents a series of cases brought to the American Court of Appeal in which elderly offenders, under the 8th Amendment, have claimed that, given their ages and life expectancies, the sentences imposed amount to life imprisonment, and are thus disproportionate to the crimes committed. For further details, see United States v. Angiulo, 852 F. Supp. 54, 60 (Mass. 1994); see also Alspaugh v. State, 133, So. 2d 597, 588 (Fla. 2d Dist. Ct. App. 1961).

[8] 533 P.2d 1151 (Ariz. 1975).

have her or his sentence reduced, s/he will experience a greater punishment than a younger person sentenced for committing the same crime. Special arrangements for elderly prisoners, such as the Angola Prison Hospice in America, can make prisons seem more like nursing homes. This raises the question of the necessity of keeping certain frail and infirm elderly persons behind bars, since the infirm elderly person is least likely to commit crimes in the future. The alternative would be to incorporate an early release scheme.[9]

It is only by exploring the possibilities that we can begin to create alternatives. At one level, it can be argued that it is only through well-funded alternatives to custody changes in sentencing, and a concerted effort to divert offenders from custody, that this can be achieved.

CONCLUSION

This chapter has highlighted how both the social construction of aging and crime is an important process in debunking discourses of 'truth' and can be used as an alternative to narrow bio-medical aging and crimogenic positivist narratives (Wahidin and Powell, 2006). This chapter has presented some of the issues and challenges of an aging prison population and questions why the criminological and gerontological imagination has been curiously silent about elders in the criminal justice system. It is only by widening the vista of the criminological and the gerontological investigation that we can begin to understand the experiences of older prisoners and bring to light the relationship between aging and crime. Second, it is by challenging the silence surrounding this particular cohort that we begin to explore the interstices of the criminological and gerontological enterprise. Thirdly, it is by questioning the purpose and nature of imprisonment in relation to this particular group that alternatives to imprisonment can be explored. It is within the reach of the criminological and the gerontological imagination to develop new alternatives

---

[9] Release on compassionate grounds in England and Wales is addressed by way of the Parole Board recommendation to the Home Secretary (and in the case of lifers through the exercise of the Royal Prerogative of Mercy). Such release may be granted on medical grounds when death is likely to occur within three months, if the prisoner is bedridden or severely incapacitated, or where further imprisonment would endanger the prisoner's life or reduce life expectancy. In 2002, France introduced a system where upon during the sentence a judge can permit the early release of the prisoner suffering from a terminal illness or whose health is incompatible with continued detention. In March 2004, 37 prisoners in the UK had applied for medical parole. Three of them who were critically ill and aged 50 and over were released (see Steiner 2003).

and imaginative solutions to the incarceration of older offenders. For example, the way forward in terms of dealing with some, if not all, older offenders is to deal with this group outside the criminal justice system so that when we talk about alternatives to imprisonment, they really do become alternatives to criminal sanctions rather than alternatives to custody. Alternatives to imprisonment and the move to curb our reliance on this institution of social order as the social historian Colin Ward, alluding to the title of Ignazio Silone's novel, 'The Seed Beneath the Snow' (1943), contends are in general:

> "...always in existence, like a seed beneath the snow, buried under the weight of the state and its bureaucracy, capitalism and its waste, privilege and its injustices...." (Ward 1973:11).

It is only by breaking the silence around the experiences and needs of offenders in later-life that this chapter has argued, why it is necessary to put older prisoners firmly in the realm of the criminological and gerontological imagination and, in turn, place the needs of this group firmly on the policy agenda. It should not be argued that women and men in later-life suffer *more* than other prisoners. The real issue is that they suffer *differently* and it is by exploring this difference that we can begin to alleviate some of the pains of imprisonment.

Chapter 3

GENDER, AGING AND THE POWER OF SPECIAL HOSPITALS

ABSTRACT

The effective provision of services and treatments for women in special hospitals is an issue of major concern for the National Health Service in the U.K. In special hospitals, women represent 20% of the patient population and yet within such institutions, the services they receive are male-based and consequently, insensitive to their needs. Furthermore, women in such regimes have been subject to emotional powerlessness, physical abuse and that current regimes are 'infantilizing, demeaning and anti-therapeutic' to them. Historically, the dominant explanatory framework relating to service delivery orientated an argument of women who required specialist treatment are in some way 'emotionally disturbed'. Consequently, the bio-psychological perspective is only one model which has dominated service provision. This paper examines women in Special Hospitals from a sociological analysis. It is clear that Bio-Psychological paradigms have dominated discussions in relation to women in special hospitals and there is an urgent need to develop other explanatory frameworks because dominant frameworks have failed to identify underlying social structures/processes/attitudes which combine to oppress and disadvantage women while simultaneously reproducing negative aspects of masculinity within prison regimes which enforce compliance with notions of 'normal femininity'.

INTRODUCTION

Today, the amount of women in Special Hospitals constitute 20%.[1,2,3] Though still low in proportion to whole gendered population of over 1, 600, it is much higher than the female prison population of 5% [4]. The greatest disproportion between the psychiatric disposals of women and men is at the least coercive end-psychiatric probation orders where the rate for women is twice that of men[5]. It is not due to decisions in court that the numbers of women in special hospitals is so high in relation to prisons, for 80% of women in special hospitals have already spent time in prison psychiatric units which suggests that the courts are failing to recognize the needs of women who are legitimately in need of psychiatric treatment, or that prison drives women 'mad',[6] or that harsh discipline is seen as an adequate treatment for 'mental illness'. In any case, there seems to be a high degree of interchangeability between the notions of prisoner and patient. Instead of Special Hospitals appealing to women as a source of help and support, they consistently fail to offer constructive treatment and the fact that a convicted woman once admitted to a special hospital loses her release date and can be detained indefinitely causes women to fear transfer no matter how bad her prison experience is[7]. In this context, there appears to be considerable confusion throughout the criminal justice system about what to do about female deviance.

The studies included in the paper derive from articles and books on female confinement generally and from feminist criminology, specifically from the available (but scarce) literature pertaining to women in special hospitals. In addition, official policy documents/inquiries have been utilized. This sociological literature review located the available relevant evidence in relation to women in special hospitals which simultaneously drew upon feminist-sociological literature on female confinement. A broader sociological perspective was warranted than reducing explanation to bio-psychological explanation which heavily utilizes the process of psychiatrization.

A significant gap in the literature, both nationally and internationally, of women's experiences in such regimes was revealed. Articles excluded from the sociological review revealed an overall concern with concepts of 'security' and 'dangerousness' without any attention to empowerment and quality of life. Sociological studies included in the review revealed an overwhelming concern with issues of disempowerment of women in special hospitals.

TREATMENTS IN SPECIAL HOSPITALS

There have been increasing concerns about the provision of treatment and services for women in Special Hospitals. This concern has been articulated by Women In Special Hospitals (WISH) that services for women are insensitive and the provision is appalling. Coupled with this, there have been concerns that services for 'mental illness' are inappropriate and genuinely not meeting the need. The Department of Health and Home Office *Review of Services for Mentally Disordered Offenders* (Reed Report) has recently highlighted the management of psychopathic and anti-social personality disorders as a topic for major consideration (Reed 1994)[8]. The final report of the working group noted the paucity of methodologically rigorous research into the effectiveness of treatment of people in Special Hospitals with such a diagnosis.

However, treatment for women with and without such diagnosis in special hospitals has been far from empowering as the Blom-Cooper report (1992) reviewed. This inquiry found that the culture at Ashworth Special Hospital was anti-therapeutic in the light of women's lives. The culture of the hospital was found to be 'macho', 'militaristic' and 'male dominated'[9]. The report posited that institutional neglect and abuse was prevalent especially as regard to women who were *'almost constantly emotionally abused and at times physically abused...they feel chronically frightened and overwhelmingly powerless'*[10]. The report concluded that *'the current regime for women is infantilizing, demeaning and anti-therapeutic. Mr Pleming for the MHAC (Mental Health Act Commission) could have been speaking for us when he stated, '...the Commission's position, I hope it is clear, that radical changes...are necessary if women in Special Hospitals are to receive the type of care which will improve their situation'*[11]. Hence, the efficacy of services for women has been highlighted as disempowering, but what is needed is a sociological literature review which transcends the historically pre-dominant bio-psychological/positivistic framework which has espoused that female offending/deviance has been related to 'dangerousness' which, in turn, explains their medical diagnosis and level of security and consequent treatment.

Special Hospitals are secure psychiatric hospitals. The statutory basis for the current special hospitals which house 'mentally disordered' people derive from the County Asylums Act (1808)[12]. In the early 19th century, 'madhouses' were built to confine the 'dangerous lunatic' and on 6 August 1860, an Act was passed for the provision of 'custody' and 'care' of "criminal lunatics" which resulted in the instigation of Broadmoor in 1863[13]. Alongside this, Rampton was opened in 1910 with Moss Side (now Ashworth) in 1914[14].

These institutions signalled the beginning of the United Kingdom policy of designing security for dangerous 'mentally disordered' people[15]. The move towards 'separate institutions' for 'dangerous' and 'non dangerous' patients emerged in the 1950's and 1960's with the development of the 'open door' philosophy in local N.H.S hospitals[16]. 'Mental Illness' was seen as akin to physical illness and special hospitals were designed to treat, not to confine, patients[17]. Research by Gostin (1986) has illustrated how the open door policy has caused intractable problems for a minority of 'less attractive' patients[18]. Many mentally disordered people were sentenced to imprisonment because courts could not find suitable placements. The governments' response to this problem was to construct more specialization. Secure units were planned in each regional authority in England and Wales. These Regional Secure Units (RSU's) are operational today. However, admission to such special hospitals are underpinned by legal categories and discretion of clinical judgements of the constitution of 'mental illness'.

ADMISSION TO A SPECIAL HOSPITAL

Officially, the Secretary of State has a duty under Section 4 of the N.H.S Act (1977) *'to provide and maintain establishments...for persons subject to detention under the Mental Health Act 1983 who, in his opinion, require treatment under conditions of special security on account of their dangerousness, violent and criminal propensities'* [19]. The hospitals established under Section 4 are entitled 'Special Hospitals': Broadmoor, Rampton and Ashworth.

The definition in Section 4 of the 1977 Act portends that special hospitals can only be used for patients liable to detention under the Mental Health Act. However, according to Gostin (1986), there have been cases where informal patients have been kept in special hospitals; for example, after a Mental Health Review Tribunal (MHRT) has discharged a patient for being liable to be detained [20]. Ironically, special hospitals are maximum security institutions which, in principle, should not house informal patients.

The term *'Special Security'* in Section 4 of the 1977 Act has been construed as meaning that it should not be less secure than that required for the most 'dangerous' (Category 'A') prisoners. In practice, the security in special hospitals is preserved by a secure parameter wall, locked wards, the 'caution' of staff and a system of constant checks [21]. Security it seems is paramount to prevent the threat of 'dangerous' individuals from harming other patients and staff.

Hence, only patients with *'dangerous, violent or criminal propensities'* should be detained in a special hospital. This means that if a patient clearly does not meet these criteria it would be unlawful to detain him/her in a Special Hospital. Yet, a study by Dell (1980) found that patients were admitted into special hospitals in spite of the Secretary of State's view that they did not require conditions of special security [22]. Special Hospitals were built as maximum security institutions for highly 'dangerous' individuals. Hence, such regimes restrict a person's freedom and quality of life. It is a 'liberty' issue which should involve the patient having basic democratic rights. Yet, the very narrow and positivistic conceptualization of the 'dangerous' patient pervades any discussion of empowerment because of 'security risk'.

According to the admission policy of Ashworth Hospital Authority, there are 3 factors which play a crucial role in admission: firstly, 'The presence or absence of recognizable mental disorder'; secondly, 'liability to detention' and thirdly, the level of 'dangerousness' [23]. The policy makes it clear that constant surveillance can only be justified when the highest levels of security are required and less security would not provide a safeguard to the public because of these 3 factors. What the Admission policy overlooks is the safeguarding of patients which was addressed by the findings of the Blom-Cooper report (1992) which found neglect, abuse, infantilization and disempowerment as pervasive among patients. It is in the context of these factors that treatments in special hospitals are operationalized.

QUESTIONING CURRENT STRUCTURES

The structure and organization around current treatments in Special Hospitals is orientated around the following: Drugs, Psychiatric treatment, Electroconvulsive therapy (ECT), Psychotherapeutic treatment, Milieu therapy, counseling and social therapy (Blom-Cooper 1992) [24]. However, a study by Stevenson (1989) has illustrated that such treatments disempower women specifically because of the overuse of drugs, for example [25]. Many women have become excessively dependent upon psychotropic drugs and which if stopped too quickly can leave women feeling more vulnerable because of the dependence upon them. In relation to ECT- where a patient is severely depressed and suicidal and the patient has given permission is seen as a last resort treatment for patients. However, Stevenson (1989) found that ECT was given to some women without consent again adding to their marginalization. ECT is seen as punishment for unacceptable behavior not as treatment or of value as empowering. Regarding Milieu therapy, this is the theory that individuals get better by virtue of being in that environment or milieu. Stevenson (1989: 16) quotes a woman in Rampton: *'When I used to work in the sewing room on the machines, they used to say that was treatment-going to that room every day and sewing'*. Arguably, this treatment epitomises feminization as proof of normalization/institutionalization. In relation to talking therapies, the principle problem identified: how can a woman patient trust the person they are talking to/being treated by when part of their job is to report on her and be her jailer? Part of the problem as McCabe (1996) identifies is that women patients feel they are not listened to [26]. There seems to be an awareness of the need for and the value of talking therapies (Blom Cooper 1992) but this has yet to operationalized (McCabe 1996; Adstead and Morris 1996; Eaton and Humphries 1996).

Much discussion of the priorities of the HSPCB (1997) is 'gender versus integrated services' [27]. One of the main critiques of the existing provision of services is how incompatible male and female services are in combination. Using the term of integration for treatments for both men and women in the context of mixed wards in hospitals is misleading as it suggests a harmonious whole. Centrally, how can women be integrated or normalized into a male environment? There are few alternatives for women to special hospitals with overcrowding being a key feature of Regional Secure Units (RSU's). Women become trapped within a system orientated around lack of alternatives coupled with a reluctance by psychiatrists to discharge women into the community. (missing super-script #28)

Indeed, since the 1970's, sociologists have developed sophisticated research methodologies on female offenders which expose the gender differentiated processes underpinning service provision and show how such processes operate in subtle yet complex ways. These studies stand in direct opposition to positivistic hypothesis testing models which attempt to quantify statistical correlations of cause and effect of criminality and levels of dangerousness [29].

CONFINEMENT

This review examined complex social processes that lay behind the categorization of female confinement and how gender assumptions/stereotypes played a pivotal feature in the subordination of such confined women in prisons/special hospitals. This review drew heavily upon historical/contemporary official documents and sociological-feminist analyses about female confinement and experiences which can be utilized to explain the marginality of women in such regimes.

GENERAL LITERATURE REVIEW OF WOMEN IN PRISONS

What the sociological literature points to is that gender stereotyping plays a crucial role in the labeling of female offending and social processing of criminalization. A study by Allen (1987) reveals that women appearing before the court are twice as likely as men to be dealt with by psychiatric means [30]. Women are more likely to be referred for psychiatric reports, more likely to be found insane or of diminished responsibility and importantly, more likely if convicted to be given psychiatric treatment at a Special Hospital in place of a penal sentence. Allen (1987) claims these findings cannot be explained by differences in the mental health of male and female offenders. Clinical judgements of 'abnormally aggressive or seriously irresponsible conduct' are applied very differently to women and men. What Allen (1987) found looking through court evidence was that the diagnosis of 'psychopath' in men was linked to the manifestation of violence; for women, fighting, thefts and sexual promiscuity were taken into account. Hence, the very application of medical classifications to men and women are prescribed via socially constructed attitudes and expectations of gender roles.

Allen's (1987) work builds upon the work of Rowett and Vaughan (1981) who found that mental institutions are devices used by dominant groups to control and regulate the behavior of unacceptable marginals [31]. Such is the social construction of medical classification, Rowett and Vaughan (1981) quote Partridge (1953) who chronicled the history of Broadmoor: *'Insanity is often brought on by child rearing...Individual pride in her personal appearance seems to be the requisite to a recovery of a woman's sanity'* [32]. Hence, pride in a feminine appearance fulfills the gender stereotype.

The work of Carlen (1983) illustrates the subjective meanings of female confinement and with particular reference to the wider meanings of the experiences of prison [33]. Carlen's (1983) study makes use of interviews with Sherrifs (Judges), police officers and social workers and utilizes observation in prisons and courts incorporating a Kaleidoscopic (diverse methods) approach. What is revealed by the talk of all those interviewed is the network of interests which underlie the logic and imagery of the judicial and penal systems when they attempt to represent the 'inadequate' woman. Carlen (1983) details the ways in which the confinement of recidivist women offenders is over-determined by the gender assumptions of law enforcers who interpret the law via discretion and consequently attach the label of 'criminal' to females. Carlen's (1983) work raises significant questions as to the meanings of imprisonment and the penal disciplining of women. Coupled with this, the use of psychiatric labels such as 'personality disorder' continues to reinforce the disempowerment of women. As Carlen (1983) has argued, although it cannot be conceptualized the application of the label makes *'women feel quite 'horribly at home' within psychiatric careers'*. Hence, normalization through psychiatry is underpinned by medical mechanisms for maintaining security. For example, there has been an increase in psychotropic drugs because *'women can be pretty wicked without the drug'* (Nursing Doctor quoted in Carlen 1983: 200). A study by Genders and Player (1987) exemplifies Carlen's research as they have indicated that between 1984 and 1985, over 145, 000 doses of anti-depressants, sedatives and tranquillizers were dispensed to women proportionately five times as many doses as men received in psychiatric units [34].

LITERATURE REVIEW OF WOMEN IN SPECIAL HOSPITALS

Special Women in Special Hospitals: Experiences

Adshead and Morris (1996) claim that women are contained in Special Hospitals because of huge discrepancies in the provision of mental healthcare [35]. These treatments (psychtropic drugs/social-psycho therapies) are unsuitable and damaging because they are designed by males for male offenders. One of the central points gathered is that women in Special Hospitals do not require the level of security offered there. Many of the women are suicidal and self-harmers with 80% of the female special hospital fitting this description and are in chronic need of therapy/empowerment- not containment/security. These authors claim that the Special Hospital like prisons brings stigmatization and a perception of a 'shameful place'. Consequently, special hospitals infantilize and punish women. They argue that levels of 'dangerousness'/perceptions of risk are not proportionate to reality. Similarly, work by McCabe (1996) has illustrated that security and containment take precedence over therapy [36]. According to her, women can become institutionalized and can expect to be in special hospitals for years which adds to stigmatization and makes rehabilitation difficult.

A study by Eaton and Humphries (1996) is one of the first to analyze the experiences of women in special hospitals [37]. These authors utilized a qualitative approach in which 15 women were interviewed from each of the special hospitals. What these authors claimed was that quantitative research would constrain women to answer set questions which does not reveal subjective experiences. Meanings and Life Histories were articulated via interview methodologies. This was a useful way of researching women as it gave respondents chances to elaborate upon experiences as opposed to measuring answers via structured/quantified questionnaires.

One of the main points gathered by Eaton and Humphries (1996) is that women must feel understood if they are to feel empowered. Empathy may help women deal with their emotions/feelings rather than self-harm. As Eaton and Humphries (1996) state, there is a fundamental need for a supportive environment.

Progress in research comes from building on the efforts who have worked before and this is exactly what the work of Hemingway (1996) illustrates.

In a collection of papers drawing from multi-disciplinary perspectives, Hemingway (1996) et al. locate the oppressive experiences of women in special hospitals [38]. Hemingway (1996) posits that women's experience of 'abuse' highlights an inability of the special hospital to protect women from physical, emotional and sexual abuse at the hands of patients and staff. While the special hospital pontificates issues of security, they consitently fail to provide security to those people inside its own regime who require it most. In addition, Hemingway (1996) claims women lack any control over their own lives and are ignored. Thus, special hospitals are not as Hemingway (1996) illustrates, so special in providing care/rehabilitation because of the distrust of patients who have been defined as 'mentally ill or ' 'dangerous'.

One of the points made by Brown and Burkett (in Hemingway 1996) is that notions of femininity and domesticity play a central role in the experiences of women patients in special hospitals. What these researchers indicate is that femininity is a factor in the control of women and as proof as re-normalization. Coupled with this, Dolan and Brand (1996) (Hemingway 1996) claim that the use of drugs is widespread and Brown (1996) claims there is little or no treatment for women who remain powerless. This paints a picture as women in special hospitals as ignored, lack any control over their own situations/lives and have few role models. In combination, Hemingway et al. locate special hospitals as anti-therapeutic and as adding to the marginality/desperation to which women feel.

DISCUSSION AND IMPLICATIONS OF THE REVIEW

It is absolutely clear from the literature review of official and unofficial documents that in the context of methodology, quantitative analysis has informed policy and practice developments via an analysis of risk and 'dangerousness' without any use of qualitative epistemology or how to improve women's situation. What is lacking from perspectives however, is a questioning of the concept of 'dangerousness' or the theorization of masculinity and its impact on women in special hospitals.

DANGEROUSNESS: IMPLICATIONS

A central question is what constitutes 'dangerousness'? Themes of individual pathology influenced by a wider familial environment has been the dominant framework which explained female dangerousness and this is highlighted by the use of milieu therapy. However, it would seem that the policy of secure specialized provision for 'dangerous' patients is based upon unfounded, yet taken for granted, assumptions. As Bowden (1985) points out 'dangerousness' is not such a clear and well-conceptualized term [39]. Hence, 'dangerousness' is not a constant, fixed personal characteristic. Rather, mentally disordered people may pose a 'risk' (Parton 1995) at certain times [40] and in response to certain situations but not in others; for example, highly vulnerable women can be 'disruptive' than very 'dangerous' in terms of behavior-r. Such labels become constructed and applied via complex processes of negotiation, classification and rapport between patients and professionals.

Hence, there is a need to transcend images of dangerousness and locate the institutional mechanisms by which women in such regimes are manipulated to facilitate perceptions of legitimated social control, masculinity and power.

However, admission to a secure institution is a self-fulfilling prophecy; patients come to be regarded as *'dangerous'*, otherwise why would they be there. It is important to recognize that all women in Special Hospitals are not fearless, manipulative and violent. Fear can be a constant factor in the daily lives of the majority of women in Special Hospitals. According to Stanko and Hobdell (1993: 27), this may often leave individuals *'isolated and unable to ask for support'* [41, 42, 43].

Worrall (1990) claims that conformity to a feminine role is negotiable; it is not an absolute requirement. It can be negotiated within the family, within communities and in the larger society, but women have to have something to negotiate with. As Worrall (1990: 34) argues, *'Class, race and age all affect the extent to which women can resist the ideological discourse of femininity'* [44]. The route by which women come to be either in court or in a Special Hospital is that someone (sometimes the woman herself) has identified their behavior as deviant and there is a requirement that they be judged as either normal/innocent or mentally abnormal/guilty (Worrall 1990). In order to draw such attention, women may have breached the terms of their negotiated feminine role or they may actually have been conforming to a negotiated feminine role not recognized by those in authority. In this way, the structural questions around the special hospital regime, its philosophy and practice are translated into individual psychological problems situated on a coping-non-coping continuum. It seems, therefore, whether as individuals or as groups, women are continually put under the microscope with every movement, gesture and response magnified and recorded by predominant 'scientific/clinical' observation.

MASCULINITY AND SPECIAL HOSPITALS

Behind the walls of the special hospital, medical personnel including psychiatrists, psychologists as well as psychiatric social workers test, probe and hypothesize about women constructing and re-constructing quantifiable profiles of the bio-psychological and narrowly conceptualized sociological factors deemed to be lying at the root of their 'instability' (Carlen 1985) [45]. Such individualized responses generates intervention into women's lives and reinforces the view that it is their problem rather than the pressurized structures and policies of the hospitals which are at fault (Adshead and Morris 1995) [46].

According to the work of Connell (1987: 187), utilizing a concept such as 'hegemony' is particularly useful in recognizing the relationship between domination and disempowerment [47]. Alternative definitions of realities and ways of behaving are not simply obliterated by power networks. Thus, while physical and psychological violence might be a cornerstone of female confinement which support dominant cultural patterns and ideologies, they are utilized within a balance of forces in which there is an everyday contestation of power and where there is always the possibility for individual, social and historical change (Connell 1987: 184) [48]. Domination is emphasised at the expense of contradiction, challenge and change both at the level individual identities (women) and social formations (staff/regimes). This position is particularly relevant for the study of women in special hospitals despite the domineering brutalization/disempowerment/infantilization which underpins and reinforces the culture of masculinity inside, this culture has often been undercut by individualist and collective strategies of dissent (WISH) and sometimes by alternative official discourses (Blom-Cooper 1992) which have provided a glimpse of the possibility for constructing social arrangements which are not built on violence and domination in such regimes.

The 'hegemonic masculinity' (Connell 1987) and the controlled use of violence which prevails in Special Hospitals with its female population exemplifies a broad pattern of physical violence, psychological intimidation which provides a stark yet chilling context in which everyday decisions are made, lives controlled and bodies and minds broken. The process of normalization and routinization underpins and gives meaning to the self-perception of the individual and the perceptions of the significant others in the power networks of the institution. As a comparison to the prison system, the work of Sim (1994) [49] makes the point that prisons sustain, reproduce and indeed intensify the most negative aspect of masculinity, molding and re-molding identities and behavioral patterns whose destructive manifestations are not left behind the walls when the prisoner (or even patient) is released. Disempowerment on the inside it seems can be mirrored on the outside.

A gendered reading of the social order and hierarchies of the female special hospital therefore moves beyond bio-psychological models and organizational imperatives or individualized profiles. What we need to point to is how the maintenance of order/security both reflects and reinforces the pervasive and deeply embedded discourses around particular forms of masculinity.

The mortification which women undoubtedly experience in their daily lives does nothing to alleviate the problems that the majority will face on their release into the community. Rather in its very *'celebration of masculinity'* (Scraton et al. 1991) [50], the Special Hospital, like other state institutions such as prisons, materially and symbolically reproduces a vision of order in which *'normal womanhood'* remains unproblematic, the template for constructing everyday social relationships between men and women prisoners/patients/professionals working with them.

CONCLUSION: MASCULINITIES AND SPECIAL HOSPITALS

Professionals who refuse to work within the bounds of accepted practices organized around discourses of power, authority and domination which underline, underpin and give meaning to the working lives of the majority of professionals/managers both on the ground and within the bureaucracy of the state. Ideologies and behavior which legitimizes disempowerment can be tied to issues of masculinity. Attempting to step outside a swamping disciplinary culture results in alienation, stress, lack of promotion and overt hostility from the majority. Potier (1995) (former member of staff at Ashworth) claims after she gave evidence to the Blom-Cooper commission, she received intimidating telephone calls at her home (Lloyd 1995).

Special Hospitals are exclusively male environments (Adshead and Morris 1995) [51]. The number of female nurses, for example, is correspondingly small. The historical development of the special hospital and the emergence of atypical culture has led to perceptions of females as *'weak'*. In contrast, an emphasis on physicality and masculinist attributes corresponds closely to what Morrison (1990) has described as a *'tradition of toughness'* [52]. This dense *'macho culture'* of Special Hospitals featured prominently in the criticisms of the recent public inquiry which, as mentioned previously, furnished an uncompromising indictment of institutional neglect and abuse. (additional text missing from superscripts in this chapter)

Chapter 4

RE-THINKING AGING, GENDER AND CRIME

This chapter explores how aging has been overlooked by perspectives within Criminology and by criminological researchers, particularly when compared to the consideration which has been given to class, race, gender and class. The aim is to demonstrate that researchers studying the relationship between older people and crime would benefit from a more careful conceptualization of 'age', one which focuses on the ways in which 'old age' itself is socially constructed, is represented and used by particular interest groups.

Criminal behavior and criminological studies have focused predominantly on young people's activities. While young people have long been associated with crime, it appears that, as is the case with social class, different age groups commit different types of crime. Yet many theories deal almost exclusively with juvenile delinquency. It has been stated that 'one of the few facts agreed on in criminology is the age distribution of crime' (Hirschi and Gottfredson, 1983:552). A series of 'moral panics' have, 'demonized young people, from the teddy boys, mods and rockers of the 1960s, through to punks, skinheads, muggers and joyriders (Curtis, 1999:28), girl gangs and mobile phone snatchers of 2000 (see, for example, Cohen, 1973; Pearson, 1983). However, the assumption that crime is overwhelmingly a young person's activity must be called into question (For a further discussion, see Wahidin 2005).

As already hinted at, up until the 1990s, the dominant criminological triumvirate of race, class and gender were seen as major vehicles that mobilied major research funding opportunities. Not only was age subsumed under race, class and gender, but the dominant explanatory framework concerning aging came from outside of criminology: bio-medicine. The medical model was and is a global influence that perceives old age, in particular, as related to physical, psychological and biological 'problems'. Such 'problems' of old age were tied to very narrow individualistic explanations, where upon aging bodies and minds 'decay' and 'decline'. Coupled with this, the rise and consolidation of functionalist accounts of old age compounded such medical discourses (Powell, 2001). For functionalists in the USA during the 1950s and 1960s, the purpose of old age was for older people to disengage from work roles and prepare for the ultimate disengagement: death (Powell, 2001). Old age then took on a problem focus. These perspectives held dominant ideas that helped shape and legitimize policies of retirement and subsequent inequality.

Indeed, 'old age' throughout the twentieth century has been seen as a social and medical problem and this predominant perspective is evident through the language used by policy makers, mass media and the general public. A significant contribution of criminology as a discipline has been to highlight how individual lives and behavior which were thought to be determined solely by biological, medical and psychological factors, are, in fact, heavily influenced by social environments in which people live. However, it is quite astonishing that given the range and explosion of such sociological ideas that there was not, until recently, much consideration and application of such critical ideas to 'aging'.

Throughout this chapter we will argue that *'criminology'* would benefit from 'aging studies' (Powell, 2001) in understanding the relationship between crime and later-life. Pain, suggests that 'age':

'... has largely been overlooked by criminologists, the debate so far being located mainly in medical and social welfare disciplines' (1997, 18).

To this end, we will map out four dimensions of: 'political economy of old age'; 'gender and aging'; 'aging and post-modernism; and 'aging and surveillance'. These areas may have overlapped with certain theories of crime and deviance but what makes this particularly illuminating and important to criminology is the rich tapestry of ideas that deconstruct aging as discursive, symbolic, experiential, material and existential subject/object of power.

We begin, by questioning the nature of *'criminology'*. We then suggest that these theories have omitted the representations of aging in their analyses and alternatively we suggest that drawing on insights from social gerontology will provide an epistemologically informed and ontologically flexible account of age, crime and society.

Hillyard et al (2004), observes that recent trends of the last ten years in criminology has been brought on by the thirst for 'evidence-led policy' research - a demand that has translated itself in the criminological context as a 'revival of number crunching, schematic and instrumental positivism' (Scraton, 2001:3). In retrospect, the decade of the 1970s appears as a watershed, in which the intellectual, institutional and political assumptions of modern criminology were challenged, often in the name of more radical social politics. It was during this decade that there arose a more critical and reflexive style of criminology, and a more explicit questioning of criminology's relation to the state, to criminal justice, and to the disciplinary processes of welfare capitalism. Criminology focused on broader themes of social thought and over time became more critical of criminal justice practice. In these years, criminology's center of gravity shifted a little, becoming more reflexive, more critical and more theoretical. 'As it happens, this was a short-lived moment [which] did not last long. Before long, new post-correctional forms of crime control emerged and criminology became immersed in applied questions once again ...' (Garland 2000, pp.13-14).

The inception of 'Critical Criminology' was in the late 1960s. Variously named 'positivism' or 'establishment criminology' was individualistic in focus, technicist in outlook and minimalist in theorizing. Its aim was the social engineering of the 'maladjusted' individual into the ranks of the value consensual society (Box, 1981). Similarly, in biomedical gerontology, such viewpoints stated that older people had traits of bodily and mental decline that shares ideas of crimogenic positivism in claiming prevalance of pathologies to explain human behavior (Wahidin and Powell, 2003). Despite the discipline of criminology having a rich imagination, the experiences of older people are excluded from the kaleidoscopic vision of the criminological gaze. What gerontological theories can criminology learn from perspectives grounded in understanding aging? Firstly, we want to take to task the very notion of 'aging' and its exclusion in mainstream criminology.

The criminological imagination regarded age as less important than race, class and gender and if discussed, focused on the question of youth. Persons in later-life were uncritically constructed as victims of crime seeped in a biomedical discourse. This construction of 'old age' tends be represented as static, portrayed as having negative connotations of physical and psychological decline coupled with social and spatial withdrawal (Bytheway, 1995). These ageist ideologies around the old age and the meaning of old age both affect and are reflected within criminology (see, in particular, the construct of victimhood and old age).

Furthermore, there has long been a tendency in matters of aging and old age to reduce the social experience of aging to its biological dimension from which a set of normative 'stages' are derived which over-determine the experience of aging of such a heterogeneous group. Accordingly, being 'old', for example, would primarily be an individualized experience of adaptation to inevitable physical and mental decline to the preparation for death (Powell, 2000).

Estes and Binney (1989) have used the expression 'biomedicalization of aging' which has two closely related narratives: one, the social construction of aging as a medical problem; two, ageist practices and social policies growing out of thinking of aging as a medical problem. They suggest:

> 'Equating old age with illness has encouraged society to think about aging as pathological or abnormal. The undesirability of conditions labeled as sickness or illness transfer to those who have these conditions, shaping the attitudes of the persons themselves and those of others towards them. Sick role expectations may result in such behaviors as social withdrawal, reduction in activity, increased dependency and the loss of effectiveness and personal control – all of which may result in the social control of the elderly through medical definition, management and treatment' (Estes and Binney, 1989, 588).

Every society uses age categories to divide this ongoing process into stages or segments of life (Cole et al, 1992). These life stages are socially constructed rather than inevitable. Aging, too, is a production of social category. At any point of a lifespan, age simultaneously denotes a set of social constructs, defined by the norms specific to a given society at a specific point in history. Thus, a specific period of life: infancy, childhood, adolescence, adulthood, middle age or old age is influenced by the structural entities of a given society. Therefore, aging is not to be considered the mere product of biological-psychological function rather a consequence of socio-cultural factors and subsequent life-chances. Indeed, society has a number of culturally and socially defined notions of what Thomas R. Cole (1992) calls the "stages of life". Historically, the stages of life were presented as a religious discourse, which formed the basis for the cultural expectations about behavior and appearance across the life-course. The life stage model is still popularly used in society which impinges on how our lives are structured albeit by bio-medical discourses of 'decline'.

In Western societies, an individuals 'age' is counted on a chronological or numerical foundation, beginning from birth to the current point of age, or when an individual has died. Chronological aging is a habit individuals engage in: 'birthdays' and 'wedding anniversaries' for example. Counting age can be seen as a social construction because it is a practice underpinned by the development of industrial capitalism (Phillipson, 1998). Hence, what is critical about aging, then, is how a society uses it to socially construct people into 'categories'. As a classificatory tool, age is important in three ways. First, like sex, age is an ascribed status or characteristic, which is, based on attributes over which we have little or no control. Second, unlike sex, a specific age is always transitional – constantly moving from one age to another and like sex is regulated by societal expectations of age-appropriate behavior. These transitions also assume that conformity is rewarded whereas deviance is punished. Thirdly, although in every society some age groups are more powerful, the unique aspect of aging is that everyone can expect to occupy various positions throughout life on the basis of his or her age.

Older people as perpetrators of crime rather than as victims of crime has been neglected in criminological discourse despite important research between the relationship between crime and ethnicity, class and gender. The academic study of corporate crime in relation to older people is scarce (Phillipson, 1998) and is as unreported as the actual corporate malpractices against older people. For example, in recent years, we have seen the effect of private pension schemes on the lives of older people: Powell and Wahidin (2004) cite a report by the Office of Fair Trading (1997) found that billions of pounds in the UK had been lost by pensioners in private pension schemes invested in corporations which The Times claimed was 'the greatest financial scandal of the century' involving corporations. Indeed, The British Financial Services Authority (1999) estimated up to £11 billion was stolen by private pension corporations which is almost three times the original estimate (Powell and Wahidin, 2004). "The number of victims could be as high as 2.4 million" (The Guardian, 13 March 1998: 13 quoted in Powell and Wahidin, 2004, 52). Coupled with this, came the discovery after the death of Robert Maxwell that he had extracted by stealth £400 million from his companies' pensions schemes (Powell and Wahidin, 2004, 55-58). Discussions of the mis-selling of pensions are replete with attributions of blame. The question that has to be addressed is why corporate crime is scarcely policed, rarely punished and how this failure contributes to facilitating this type of crime against older people in particular and 'aging populations' in general?

THEORIZING AGING STUDIES –
AGE, GENDER, IDENTITY AND SURVEILLANCE

Old age is shamefully seen like head lice in children and venereal disease in their older siblings (Stott, 1981: 3).

One of the major problems in 'Criminology' in recent years is that the study of aging has not been developed. Theoretical developments in Critical Criminology pertaining to older people have lagged well behind other social and human science disciplines. George (1995) argues that one of the reasons for this invisibility is that gerontological research is seen as "theoretically sterile". In other words, why would anyone want to research experiences of older people and crime? Secondly, the neglect of later-life issues within criminology is that youth as with the study of offenders unleashes the voyeur. In contrast, the study of old age and crime as Pollak (1941), astutely observed approximately 60 years ago, evokes a different reaction:

> 'Old criminals offer an ugly picture and it seems as if even scientists do not like to look at it for any considerable amount of time…..On the other hand, if the thesis of the inter-relationship between age and crime is to hold, an investigation of all its implications has to yield results, and with the tendency of our population to increase in the higher age brackets, a special study of criminality of the aged is required' (1941:212).

Notwithstanding this, the emergence of the social theories of age and aging can be located to the early post-war years with the governmental concern about the consequences of demographic change and the shortage of younger people in work in the US and the UK (Biggs & Powell, 2001). In the post-war years, social gerontology emerged as a multi-disciplinary field of study which attempted to respond to the social, health and economic policy implications and projections of population change (Phillipson, 1998). The wide disciplinary subject matter of social gerontology was shaped by significant external forces: first, by state intervention to achieve specific outcomes in health and social policy for older people; secondly, by a socio-political and economic environment which viewed an aging population as an emerging 'social problem' for western society (Phillipson, 1998). The important point to note is that theories often mirror the norms and values of their creators and their social times, reflecting culturally dominant views of what should be the appropriate way to analyze social phenomena (Turner, 1989). Critical gerontology explains adult aging and how the assumptions contained within theory and policy influence our understanding of the position of older people in society.

Many of the gerontological texts provide an historical understanding of the development of the gerontological field from the first demographic studies conducted in the mid 1940s to the most recent genre, that until now has omitted gender issues (Arber & Ginn, 1995; Bernard & Meade 1993; Ginn and Arber 1995). Throughout the gerontological literature of the last decade, it is emphasized that the voices and needs of older persons have to be integrated into policy, and that such policy must not be steeped in the stereotypes of aging but must acknowledge and assess diversity and difference.

James Birren makes the point that the study of aging, or gerontology as it is called, is 'data rich and theory poor'. Bengston et al (1997) argues that the study of aging has lacked a strong theoretical core and has tended to ignore, until recently, an understanding of aging identity, the body, cultural representations of aging to name a few, which are central features of an emerging post-modern paradigm in gerontological theory. While a significant amount of data has been generated over the years (around issues such as health and social needs in old age), there has been a lack of theoretical discussion of the meaning and place of aging within the structure of society.

The role of theory in gerontology and its growth as a discipline coincides with the post-war years; a growth in public awareness and interest in aging issues; from 'Grey Power movements' to the aging population, the crisis over pensions and the funding of the welfare state (Aiken, 1995; Phillipson, 1998). Nevertheless, the lack of theoretical integration in British gerontology has been a cause of some anxiety over the last twenty years (Biggs, 1999). Fennell, Phillipson and Evers comment: 'Much more characteristic of British research is the lack of attention to theory of any kind. This failing has been a feature of the social gerontological tradition (1993:42). The pressures on older people in the workplace combined with the rapid growth in early retirement have resulted in a significant shift in the way aging is experienced and perceived' (Achenbaum, 1978).

Gubrium & Wallace (1990) seek to promote the development of gerontological theory by posing the question 'who theorizes age?' Their focus suggests that it is not only professional social gerontologists who theorize age; we all are involved in constructing the 'other' in relation to ourselves. Critical gerontology is concerned with '..... a collection of questions, problems and analyses that have been excluded by established [mainstream gerontology]' (Fennell, Phillipson & Evers, 1993:13). These vary from questions about the role of the state in the management of old age (Phillipson, 1982, 1998;

Phillipson & Walker, 1986b; Townsend,1962,1981) to issues about the purpose of growing old within the context of a post-modern life course (Cole, 1992; Featherstone, 1995). Critical gerontology seeks to problematize the construction of aging and to identify the conditions experienced by elders in society (Phillipson, 1998). We now turn our attention to gerontological approaches which provide some evocative conceptual tools for criminologists to ponder: political economy of aging; gender and aging; aging and post-modernism and aging and surveillance.

Critical Gerontology

Political Economy of Old Age emerged as a critical theory in both sides of the Atlantic. Political economy drew from Marxian insights in analyzing the capitalist society and how old age was socially constructed to foster the needs of the economy (Estes 1979). This critical branch of Marxist gerontology grew as a direct response to the hegemonic dominance of structural functionalism in the form of disengagement theory, the biomedical paradigm and world economic crises of the 1970s. As Phillipson (1998), points out, in the UK huge forms of social expenditure were allocated to older people. Consequently, not only were older people viewed in medical terms but in resource terms by governments. This brought a new perception to attitudes to age and aging. As Phillipson states:

> 'Older people came to be viewed as a burden on western economies, with demographic change... seen as creating intolerable pressures on public expenditure' (1998: 17).

Hence, the major focus is an interpretation of the relationship between aging and the economic structure. In the US, Political Economy theory was pioneered via the work of Estes (1979), and Estes, Swan and Gerard (1982). Similarly, in the UK, the work of Walker (1981) and Phillipson (1982) added a critical sociological dimension to understanding age and aging in advanced capitalist societies. For Estes (1979), political economy challenges the ideology of older people as belonging to a homogenous group unaffected by dominant structures in society. Estes (1979) claims political economy focuses upon an analysis of the state in contemporary societal formations. Estes looks to how the state decides and dictates who is allocated resources, who is not and why. This, in turn, has direct implications on retirement, pensions and the health and social care needs of the older population (Powell and Wahidin, 2004). As Phillipson (1982) points out, the retirement experience is linked to the timing of economic reduction of wages and enforced withdrawal from work has put many older people in the UK in a financially insecure position. Hence, the state can make and break the 'minds and hearts of its populace' (Biggs and Powell, 2001). Phillipson (1982, 1986) considers how capitalism helps to socially construct the social marginality of older people in key areas such as welfare delivery. The important argument Phillipson (1998) makes is that inequalities in the distribution of resources should be understood in relation to the distribution of power within society, rather than in terms of individual variation. Similarly, in the US, Estes, Swann and Gerard (1982) claims that the state is using its power to transfer responsibility for welfare provision from the state and onto individuals.

Gender and Aging

Feminist theorizing is one of the most significant areas of theoretical development in approaches to aging (Arber & Ginn 1991, Ginn and Arber 1995). There are two important issues: first, power imbalances shape theoretical construction; second, a group's place within the social structure influences theoretical attention they are afforded. Henceforth, because older women tend to occupy a position of lower class status, especially in terms of economic status than men of all ages and younger women, they are given less theoretical attention (Arber & Ginn, 1995). According to Acker (1988 cited in Arber and Ginn 1991), in all known societies the relations of distribution and production are influenced by gender and thus take on a gendered meaning. Gender relations of distribution in capitalist society are historically rooted and are transformed as the means of production change. Similarly, age relations are linked to the capitalist mode of production and relations of distribution. "Wages" take on a specific meaning depending on age. For example, teenagers work for less money than adults, who, in turn, work for less money than middle-aged adults. Furthermore, young children rely on personal relations with family figures such as parents. Many older people rely on resources distributed by the state.

Older women are viewed as unworthy of respect or consideration (Arber and Ginn 1991). Arber and Ginn (1991) claim there is a double standard of aging as arising from the sets of conventional expectations as to age-pertinent attitudes and roles for each sex which apply in patriarchal society. These are defined by Itzin as a male and a female 'chronology', socially defined and sanctioned so that the experience of prescribed roles is sanctioned by disapproval. Male chronology, and identity is constructed around employment and the public sphere, but a woman's age status is defined in terms of events in the reproductive cycle.

It is perhaps emblematic of contemporary western society that aging marginalizes the experiences of women through an inter-connected oppression of gender and aging. The reason for this as Arber and Ginn (1991) claim, is that patriarchal society exercises power through the chronologies of employment and reproduction, and through the sexualized promotion of a 'youthful' appearance in women.

The point of a feminist analysis in gerontology is to point to the experiences and identities of *older* women. In relation to the study of crime, the exclusion of older women by feminist writers such as Heidensohn (1985) and Carlen and Worrall (1987) have focused exclusively on younger women's experiences of criminal justice. However, research on older people in the criminal justice system is very slowly being addressed by a handful of writers such as Helen Codd (1998), Judith Phillips (1996) and Azrini Wahidin (2004).

An examination of sex ratios as age increases highlights the feminisation of later-life (See Office of Population Census and Surveys 2005). The imbalance in the numbers of older men and women has a number of consequences, particularly in terms of marital status and living arrangements. Due to increase longevity, and the tendency for men to marry women younger than themselves, women are more likely to experience widowhood. Fewer women than men remarry following widowhood or divorce and consequently more older women than older men live alone. At present, half of women 65 years and over and a fifth of older men live alone. In addition, given the predominance of women among the 'very old', they are more likely to live with others and in institutional settings (Arber and Ginn, 1995). Therefore, it has been argued, the older population remains vulnerable to certain types of crime, especially domestic violence (Pain, 1997) and elder abuse. Accordingly, if the domestic victimization of older people is understood in a power relations framework, patriarchy is (at least) a joint suspect with ageism. Parallels have been drawn between ageism and sexism elsewhere, as feminist modes of inquiry, analysis and theorization provide useful lessons for the conceptualization of age (Arber and Ginn, 1995; Laws, 1995). Ageism involves not only a different set of cultural stereotypes of older women (mostly more negative than those of older men), but a different set of relations between older women and the social and economic system.

As Pain (1997, 6) points out:

'Theorizing age parallels the theorizing of gender to some extent. Age. as well as gender, structures *what* behaviors become criminal, and when certain behaviors become defined as criminal … Importantly, a high proportion of elder abuse victims are female, and offenders are usually male'.

Notwithstanding this, while feminist inquiry is useful to the victimization of older people, there is a danger in assuming that age is much 'the same type of thing' as gender. Uncritical applications of one body of knowledge/theory onto another never works out well, and there are problems with simplistic parallels between elder abuse, domestic violence and child abuse.

Elder abuse in formal or institutional care is the most likely of all to involve a female abuser, as caregivers as well as clients are overwhelmingly female. Aitken and Griffin comment that this is 'a scenario which defies gender stereotypes and is therefore addressed through the pathologising of the individual - a move commonly used in relation to women who are regarded as transgressing gendered boundaries - or not addressed at all' (Aitken and Griffin, 1996: 11). Their own work in Northamptonshire supports the existence of a male-dominated pattern of abuse in informal care (within the home), finding that abusers are most often male, more often sons than husbands.

Aging in Postmodernity

In the 1990s, there has been a vast interest in post-modern perspectives of age and aging identity underpinned by discourses of "better lifestyles" and increased leisure opportunities for older people due to healthier lifestyles and increased use of bio-technologies to facilitate the longevity of human experiences (Featherstone & Hepworth 1993). The intellectual roots of 'post-modern gerontology' derive from Jaber F. Gubrium's (1975) discovery of the Alzheimer's disease in the US and the establishment of boundaries between 'normal' and pathological aging: old age is seen as a "mask" which conceals the essential identity of the person beneath. The view of the aging process as a mask/disguise concealing the essentially youthful self beneath is one which appears to be a popular argument (Featherstone & Hepworth 1993).

There are two underlying issues for Featherstone and Hepworth (1993) which should be understood as the basis for understanding post-modern gerontology. Firstly, the mask alerts social gerontologists to the possibility that a tension exists between the external appearance of the body and face and functional capacities and the internal or subjective sense of experience of personal identity which is likely to become prominent as we age.

Secondly, older people are usually 'fixed' to roles without resources which does not do justice to the richness of their individual experiences and multi-facets of their personalities. Idealistically, Featherstone and Hepworth (1993) argue that a post-modern perspective would deconstruct such realities and age should be viewed as fluid with possibilities not constrained by medical model decline discourses.

The point of this analysis is not to accept fixed discourses of aging as represented by victimization or that older people are a homogenous group. There is an ontological flexible narrative to the diversity and richness of older people's lives that transcend limited bio-medical and common sense assumptions of the problems faced by persons in later-life.

Aging and Surveillance State

For older people, especially within carceral institutions, life is organized around the operational needs of the total institution (Wahidin and Powell, 2004), and all movement is under surveillance. Similar to residential homes, on admission they experience distress and depression not only from the transition away from the familiarities of home but to being positioned in a state of dependency (Wahidin and Powell, 2004). At the same time, the voices of professionals become louder and older people's voices are rendered silent in the landscape of power/knowledge and the politics of social relations. To exemplify this, Clough (1988) completed a study of abuse at a residential care home in England. He found that many staff in his study neglected older residents by failing to bathe residents and removing blankets from residents which led to pneumonia. Vousden (1987 cited in Hadley and Clough, 1995) claimed that professionals surveillance practices destroyed the positive identity of many older people in such a repressive residential regime:

'It is self-evident that when elderly, often confused residents are made to eat their own feces, are left unattended, are physically man-handled or are forced to pay money to care staff and even helped to die, there is something seriously wrong' (Vousden, 1987 quoted in Hadley and Clough, 1995, 63).

Hence, the power/knowledge twist of professional 'carergivers' was detrimental to policy statements concerning "choice" and "quality of life" in residential care. Such care action was a powerful and a repressive mechanism used to indent and strip the identities of residents – and yet this has been seen as a social welfare issue rather than an issue of criminal justice.

It is the risky, unfixed character of modern life that underlies our accelerating concern with control and crime control in particular. It is not just crime that has changed; society has changed as well, and this transformation has reshaped criminological theory, social policy and the cultural meaning of crime and criminality.

CONCLUSION

The aim of this chapter has been to connect aging studies to criminology and to argue that criminologists studying the relationship of crime and later-life have to turn to gerontological literature and move from either ignoring the area and, at worst, be accused of replicating ageist discourse. New roles are emerging for older people in the developed West around work, family, leisure, criminal activity etc. challenging the expectations and roles of older people in society. Critical gerontology can inform criminology from an age-awareness perspective bringing a more complex understanding to the experiences of crime and later-life. (For further explanation of the integration of gerontolgical and criminological theory, see Wahidin's work on older male and females experiences of prison 2004, 2005).

These gerontological theories cited have been at the forefront of understanding old age in the US, UK and Australian academies. Taken together, these theoretical currents have been influential in providing gerontology with a rich social dimension. Such social theories have been used also to analyze pressing social issues such as, elder abuse, the gendered nature of age, the politics of power relations between older people and state/society and community care. The purpose of this chapter has been to amalgamate the key ideas of social theories of age in order to stress the importance of aging to understanding age, crime and society. No longer can criminologists ignore the importance of gerontological theory in the study of old age and crime. The absence of older offenders in the criminological imagination mirrors where the study of female offenders in criminology was forty years ago. The lack of research in this area is an implicit form of ageism that implies that the problems of this group can be disregarded, or that aging criminals are simply not worth discussing. By denying elders who are caught in the criminal justice system, a voice and, in turn, neglecting this area as a legitimate area of research criminology indirectly replicates ageism and reproducing the hierarchy of power that excludes and invalidates the experiences of an aging population.

BIBLIOGRAPHY

Age Concern (1980) Crime Prevention: Action Against Crime, London, England.

Antunes G. E, Cook F.L , Cook T.D . Skogan, W.G (1977), Patterns of Personal Crime Against the Elderly: *Findings from a National Survey in Gerontologist,* 17, 321-327.

Baldassare M. (1986), *The Elderly and Fear of Crime*, Sociology and Social *Research,* 70, 218-221.

Bennett, G, *Kingston, P and Penhale B (1997),* The Dimensions of Elder Abuse, Palgrave Macmillan

Biggs, S (1993), Understanding Aging: Images, Attitudes and Professional Practice, Buckingham: Open University Press.

Box S, Hale, C, and Andrews, G. (1986), Fear of Crime: Causes, Consequences and Control, University of Kent Applied Statistics Research Unit Report to the Home Office.

Box, S, Hale, C, and Andrews, G (1988), Explaining Fear of Crime, *British Journal of Criminology*, Vol 28. No 3 Summer 340 – 356.

Braungart, M. M., Braugart, R.G, and Hoyer, W. J, (1980) *Age, Sex and Social Factors in Fear of Crime, Sociological Focus,* 13, 55-66.

Brogden, M & Nighar, P (2000), Crime, Abuse and the Elderly, Cullumpton, Willan.

Chivite-Matthews, N. and Maggs, P. (2002) Crime, Policing and Justice: the experience of older people. London: Home Office.

Clarke, A. H and Lewis, M (1982), Fear of Crime Among the Elderly, *British Journal of Criminology,* 22, 49-69

Coleman, R. (2004) Reclaiming the Streets: Surveillance, *Social Control and the City.* Willan.

Davis, P, Francis, P, and Jupp V. (eds) (2003), Victimology, Victimization and Public Policy in P. Davis et al (eds), *Victimisation, Theory, Research and Policy*, London, Macmillan Press.

Dobash R and Dobash R. (1992), Women, Violence and Social Change. London: Routledge

Dobash, R.P. and Dobash R.E. (2004) Women's Violence to Men in Intimate Relationships:Working on a Puzzle'. *British Journal of Criminology.* 44:324-349.

Elias R. (1986), The Politics of Victimization. Oxford, Oxford University Press.

Estes, C, Biggs, S and Phillipson, C (2004) Social Theory, Aging and Social Policy, OUP: Milton Keynes

Fattah E (1993) Victimization and Fear of Crime among the Elderly: *A possible link? Australian Institute of Criminology*

Fattah, E. A. and Sacco, V.F (1989), *Crime and Victimization of the Elderly.* New York: Springer.

Fattah, E.A (1991), Understanding Criminal Victimization Scarborough, Ont, Prentice-Hall.

Fattah, S. (1995), Crime and Older People - Victimization and Fear of Crime among the Elderly: A Possible link? *Australian Institute of Criminology.*

Giles-Sims, A. (1984), *A Multi-variate Analysis of Perceived likelihood of Victimization and Degree of Worry about Crime among Older People, Victimology,* 9, 222-233

Gordon, M.T, Rigers, S. LeBailey, R. K and Heath L. (1980), *Crime, Women and the Quality of Urban Life, Signs,* 5, 144-160.

Gubrium, J.F. (1974), *Victimization in Old Age: Available Evidence and Three Hypotheses, Crime and Delinquency,* 20, 245-250.

Hale, C. (1996), *Fear of Crime: A Review of the Literature, International Review of Victimology,* 4: 79-150.

Hallett, M. (1994), *'Why we fail at crime control', Peace Review, Summer,* pp. 177-81.

Hentig, H. von (1948), The Criminal and his Victim, New Haven: Yale University Press.

Home Office (1999) A Question Of Evidence? *Investigating And Prosecuting Rape In The 1990s.* London: HMSO.

Hughes G. (1991) Understanding Crime Prevention, Oxford, Oxford University Press.

Jones, G. M. (1987), Elderly People and Domestic Crime, in the *British Journal of Criminology,* Vol. 27, 191-201.

Malinchak, A, A. (1980), Crime and Gerontology. *Englewood Cliffs,* NJ: Prentice Hall.

Mawby R. and Walklate S. (1994), Critical Victimology: *The Victim in International Perspective*, London: Sage.

Mawby, R. (1988), 'Age Vulnerability and the Impact of Crime' in M. Maguire and J. Pointing (eds), Victims of Crime: A New Deal? Milton Keynes: Open University Press, 101-11.

Mendelsohn B. (1963), *The Origin and Doctrine of Victimology Excerpta Criminolgical,* Vol 3 (May- June): 239:44.

Mirrlees-Black, C. and Allen, J. (1998), Concern about Crime: Findings from the 1998 British Crime Survey Research Findings No.83, *Research Development and Statistics Directorate.* London Home Office.

Mirrlees-Black, C. Budd, T,. Partridge, S. and Mayhew P. (1998), The 1998 British Crime Survey Home Office Statistical Bulletin, 21/98 Home Office London.

Moore, M.H. and Trojanowitcz R.C (1988) Policing and the Fear of Crime Perspectives Policing 3. U.S Dept of Justice Washington.

Pain, R. (1997), 'Old age' and Ageism in Urban Research: The Case of Fear of Crime' , *International Journal of Urban and Regional Research,* 21,1,117-28.

Pain, R. (2003), Old Age and Victimization in P. Davis et al (eds) Victimization, Theory, Research and Policy, London, Macmillan Press.

Pantazis, C. (2000) 'Fear of Crime', Vulnerability and Poverty: Evidence from the British Crime Survey. *British Journal of Criminology* 40, 414-436.

Phillipson, C. (1982), Capitalism and the Construction of Old Age, London: Macmillian.

Phillipson, C., and Walker, A. (eds) (1986), Aging and Social Policy, A Critical Assessment: Aldershot, Gower.

Pollak, O. (1941), *'The Criminality of Old Age' Journal of Criminal Psychotheraphy,* 3, 213-235.

Powell, J (2001), 'Theorizing Gerontology: The Case of Social Policy, Old Age and Professional Power in UK', *Journal of Aging & Identity,* 6, (3), 117-135.

Stott, M (1981) Aging for Beginners, Oxford: Blakewell

Skogan, W. G. (1987) 'The Impact of Victimization on Fear'. *Crime and Delinquency,* 33: 135-154.

Sparks, R Genn H and Dodd, D. (1977), Surveying Victims , Chichester: Wiley.

Sparks, R (1992) Television and the Drama of Crime: Moral Tales and the Place of Crime in Moral Life. Open University Press, Buckingham

Taylor, R.B. and Hale, C. (1986), Testing Alternative Models of Fear of Crime *Journal of Criminal Law and Criminology,* 77 151-189.

Thomas C.W. and Hyman J.M. (1977), Perceptions of Crime, Fear of Vicitimization, and Public Perceptions of Police Performance in the *Journal of Police Science and Administration*, 5, 305-317.

Toseland, R. (1982), Fear of Crime: Who is the Most Vulnerable *Journal of Criminal Justice* 10, 199-209.

Turner, B. (1988), 'Aging, Status Politics and Sociological Theory' in *The British Journal of Sociology,* Vol 40, No 4: 589-605.

Twigg, J. (2004) 'The Body, Gender and Age: Feminist insights in Social Gerontology', *Journal of Aging Studies* 18. 59-73.

Von Hentig H (1948) The Criminal and his Victim, Yale University Press

Walby, S. and Allen, J. (2004) 'Domestic violence, sexual assault and stalking: Findings from the British Crime Survey'. Home Office Research Study 276. London: Home Office.

Walker, A. (1985), The Care Gap: How Can Local Authorities meet the Needs of the Elderly? London: Local Government Information Unit.

Warr, M (1985), Fear of Rape Among Urban Women Social Problems, 32,238-50.

Yin, P.P (1985), Fear of Crime as a Problem for the Elderly, Social Problems Vol 30 240-245.

REFERENCES

Acoca, L. (1998) 'Defusing the Time Bomb: Understanding and Meeting the Growing Healthcare Needs of Incarcerated Women in America' in *Crime and Delinquency,* 44, 49-70.

Aday, R. (1994a), Aging in Prison: A Case Study of New Elderly Offender in International Journal Of Offender Therapy and Comparative Criminology, Vol.1, Part 38: 79-91.

Aday, R. (1994b), Golden Years Behind Bars: Special Programs and Facilities for Elderly Inmates in Federal Probation 58: 2: 47-54.

Aday, R.H. (1995) A Preliminary Report on Mississippi's Elderly Prison Population. Parchment, MS: Mississippi's Department of Corrections.

Aday, R. H. (1999) 'Golden Years Behind Bars: A Ten-Year Follow Up'. Paper presented at the annual meeting of the Academy of Criminal Justices Sciences, Orlando, FL.

Aday, R.H. (2001) A Comprehensive Health Assessment of Aged and Infirm Inmates. Nashville, TN: Tennessee Department of Correction.

Aday, R.H , Farnely, L and Wahidin A (2006),

Aday, R., and Webster, E. (1979), Aging in Prison: The Development of a Preliminary Model in Offender Rehabilitation 3: 1979: 271-282.

Aday R H (2003), Aging Prisoners: Crisis in American Corrections. Westport CT: Praeger Publishers

Aday, R. H., Krabil, L., and Wahidin, A. (2004) *A Comparative Study of Healthcare Needs of the Female Aging Offender in the USA and the UK,* American Society of Criminology Conference 2004, Nashville. Unpublished paper.

Aday, R. H., Farney, L., and Wahidin, A. (2006)

American Correctional Association. (2003). *Adult and juvenile directory*. Lanham, Maryland.

Anno, B.J, Graham, C., Lawrence, J. and Shandsky, R. (2004) Correctional Health Care: Addressing the Needs of Elderly, Chronically Ill and Terminally Ill Inmates. Washington, D.C: National Institute of Corrections, US Department of Justice.

Anderson, J.C and Morton, J.B (1989) 'Graying of the Nation's Prisons Presents New Challenges', The Aging Connection, 10:6.

Bauman, Z. (2000) *Liquid Modernity*, London: Polity Press.

Beck, A J. (1997). Growth, change and stability in the U.S. prison population, 1980-1995.

Bengston, V., Burgess, E, & Parrott, T. (1997). 'Theory, Explanation and a Third Generation of Theoretical Development in Social Gerontology', *Journal of Gerontology: Social Sciences*, 52 (B), 72-88.

Biggs, S. (1993), *Understanding Aging - Images, Attitudes and Professional Practice:* Buckingham: Open University Press.

Biggs. S. (1999). *The Mature Imagination*. Milton Keynes: OUP

Bond, J., Briggs, R., and Coleman, P. (1993b), 'The Study of Aging', in J. Bond, P, Coleman, and S. Peace (eds), (1983), *Aging in Society - An Introduction to Social Gerontology:* London: Sage.

Byock, I.R. (2002) 'Dying Well in Corrections: Why Should We Care?', *Journal of Correctional Health Care,* 12: 27-35.

Bytheway, B. (1994), *Ageism.* Buckingham: Open University Press.

Cohen, S. (1973) *Folk Devils and Moral Panics*, Oxford: Martin Robertson.

Cole, T (1992) The Journey of Life, New York: Cambridge University Press

Colsher, P.L. , Wallace, R.B, Loeffelhotz, P.L. and Sales, M (1992) 'Health Status of Older Male Prisoners: A Comprehensive Survey', *American Journal of Public Health,* 82: 881-84.

Curtis, S (1999) Children who Break the Law: London Waterside Press.

Cullen, F., Wozniak, J., and Frank J., (1985), The Rise of the New Elderly Offender: Will a New Criminal Be Invented? In *Crime And Social Justice* Vol 23, 151-165.

Douglass, R.L. (1991) Old-Timers: Michigan's Elderly Prisoners. Langsing, Michigan: Michigan Department of Corrections.

Fazel, S, Hope T, O'Donnell, I and Jacoby, R (2001). Hidden Psychiatric Morbidity in Elderly Prisoners, *British Journal of Psychiatry*

Fennell, G,. Phillipson, C., Evers, H. (1993), *The Sociology of Old Age:* Milton Keynes, Open University Press.

Florida Corrections Commission (2001) *Annual Report Section: Status Report on Elderly Offenders*. Tallahassee FL: Florida Corrections Commission.

Flynn E. (1992) 'The Graying of America's Prison Population', *The Prison Journal,* 16: 77-98.

Flynn, E (2000) Elders as Perpetrators in M..Rothman, B. Dunlo and P. Entzel 9eds) Elders, Crime and the Criminal justice System , New York: Springer.

Gallagher, E. (1990) 'Emotional, Social, and Physical Health Characteristics of Older Men in Prison', *International Journal of Aging and Human Development*: Vol. 31 (4): 251-265.

Gallagher, E. (1990), 'Emotional, Social, and Physical Health Characteristics of Older Men in Prison' in the *International Journal of Aging and Human Development*:Vol.31 (4): 251-265.

Garland, D (2002) 'Of Crimes and Criminals: The Development of Criminology in Britain', in M. Maguirel , R. Morgan and R, Reiner (eds), The Oxford Handbook of Criminology , 3rd edn, pp. 7-50. Oxford: Oxford University Press.

Goetting, A. (1992) 'Patterns of Homicide Among the Elderly', *Violence and Victims:* 7, 203-215.

Hammack, B.W. (26 September 2004), 'Aging Prisoners Behind Bars', Roanoke times, P. A1.

Hillyard, P., Sim, J., Tombs, S. Whyte, D. (2004) 'Leaving a "Stain Upon the Silence': Contemporary Criminology and the Politics of Dissent' in the *British Journal of Criminology,* 4 (3).

Hirschi T and Gottfredson, M (1983) 'Age and the Explanation of Crime, *American Journal of Sociology,* 89:552-84

Hood, R (2004) ' Hermann Mannheim and Max Grunhut - Criminological Pioneers in London and Oxford', *British Journal of Criminology,* 4 (44) : 469-95.

James, M. (1992), 'Sentencing of Elderly Criminals' in *American Criminal Law Review* Vol, 29:1025-1044.

Kratcoski, P.C & Babb, S (1990) 'Adjustment for Older Inmates: An Analysis by Institutional Structure and Gender*'* in the *Journal of Contemporary Criminal Justice*, 6 139-156

Mezey, M, Dubler, N.N, Mitty E amd Brody,A.A. (2002) 'What Impact do Setting and Transitions Have on the Quality of Life at the End of Life and Quality of the Dying Process? *The Gerontologist,* 42 Special Issue III, pp. 54-67.

Moritz, J. (21 March 2004) Elderly Inmates Costing Millions, Ft. Worth Star Telegram, p.p1 , 1A.

National Institute of Corrections (1997) Prison Medical Care: Special Needs of Populations and Cost Control, Longmont CO.

Newman, E. (1984) 'Elderly Offenders and American Crime' in E. Newman, D. Newman, M. Gewirtz (eds) *Elderly Criminals,* Cambridge: Gunn and Hain, Publishers Inc.

Neff, J (1997) The Old's Folk's Slammer, World Press Review, 44 (2): 30-4.

NOMS (2007) Prison Population and Accommodation Briefing, London November 23.

Pain R. H. (1997), 'Old Age and Ageism in urban Research: The Case of the Fear of Crime'*, International Journal of Urban and Regional Research,* 21 (1):16-35

Pearson,G (1983) Hooligan: A History of Respectable Fears. Basingstoke: Macmillan.

Phillips J (1996),'Crime and Older Offenders', Practice 8 (1): 43-55

Phillips, J. (2005) 'Crime and Older People: The Research Agenda' in A. Wahidin and M. Cain (eds) *Aging, Crime and Society*, Cullompton: Willan.

Powell, J (2006) *Social Theory and Aging*. Rowman and Littlefield: New York

Prison Reform Trust (2003) Growing Old in Prison, London, Prison Reform Trust

Prison Reform Trust (2007)*Prison Reform Trust Factfile,* PRT: London

Prison Reform Trust (2004) *Prison Reform Trust Factfile,* PRT: London.

Radzinowicz, L. (1988) The Cambridge Institute of Criminology: Its *Background and Scope.* London: HMSO.

Radiznowicz, L (1999) Adventures in Criminology. London: Routledge.

Shimkus, J (2004) *Corrections Copes with care for the Aged, Correct Care,* 18 (3): 1, 16.

The Times (2004) German Pensioners Turn to Crime: 16th November 2004.

Townsend, P (1981) ' The Structured Dependency of the Elderly: *Creation of Social Policy in the Twentieth Century, Aging and Society,* 1: 5-28

Turley, J (1990) 'Long-Term Confinement and the Aging Inmate Population', U.S. Department of Justice, Federal Bureau of Prisons, Form on Issues in Corrections, 'Alternative Solutions'

Wahidin A (2005b) 'Older Offenders, Crime and the Criminal Justice System' in C. Hale, K.Hayward, A. Wahidin and E. Wincup (eds) *Criminology,* Oxford, Oxford University Press.

Wahidin A and Cain, M (eds) (2006) Aging, Crime and Society, Cullumpton, Willan.

Wahidin, A. (2002) 'Reconfiguring Older Bodies in the Prison Time Machine', *Journal of Aging and Identity* 7 (3):177-193.

Wahidin, A (2004) Older Women in the Criminal Justice System Running Out of Time London: Jessica Kingsley

Wahidin, A. (2005a) 'Older Offenders, Crime and the Criminal Justice System', in C. Hale, K. Hayward, A. Wahidin & E. Wincup (eds) *Criminology*, Oxford: Oxford University Press.

Wahidin, A. (2005b) *Managing the Needs of Older Offenders: Re-awakening the Criminological Imagination*, Leeds University, British Society of Criminology: Unpublished paper.

Wahidin, A and Powell, J (2006) 'Re-thinking Criminology: The Case of Aging Studies'. In Wahidin, A and Cain, M. (Eds) *Aging, Crime and Society*. Willan

Walker, A and Naeghele, G (Eds.) (1999) *The Politics of Old Age in Europe*, Milton Keynes: OUP

Ward, C (1973) Anarchy in Action. London: Allen & Unwin.

Ware, S (2007) The Care and welfare of older people in prison: a service user perspective, Age Concern England, London Unpublished Report.

Yates, J and Gillespie, W (2000) 'The Elderly and Prison Policy', *Journal of Aging and Social Policy,* 11 (2-3): 167-76.

INDEX